FOUR DAYS
FROM
FORT WINGATE

FOUR DAYS FROM FORT WINGATE:

The Lost Adams Diggings
by
Richard French

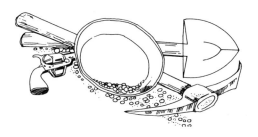

The Caxton Printers, Ltd.
Caldwell, Idaho
1994

Library of Congress Cataloging-in-Publication Data

French, Richard, 1931–
    Four days from Fort Wingate : the Lost Adams diggings / by
Richard French
       p.   cm.
    Includes bibliographical references and index.
    ISBN 0-87004-362-5 : $9.95
    1. Southwest, New--Gold discoveries.   2. Gold mines and mining-
Southwest, New--History--19th century.   3. Legends--Southwest,
New.
I. Title.
F786.F797   1994
979--dc20
                                      94-32395
                                          CIP

Photographs and Illustrations
Provided by the Author

Cover Design by Teresa Sales

Line art by E.L. Reedstrom
and Teresa Sales

Lithographed and bound in the United States of America by
The CAXTON PRINTERS, Ltd.
Caldwell, ID 83605
158382

To Lois

TABLE OF CONTENTS

FOREWORD

Few words in the languages of mankind stir imaginations and cause hearts to beat faster than the word *gold*. Perhaps this highly valued mineral is responsible for more joy, pain, frustration, and danger than any other single, tangible source. The dream, the pursuit, and the possession of gold have led many along a path to disappointment and even death. Nevertheless, the lure of the unknown and the promise of wealth continue to call the adventurous to try their hand in the quest.

In this story, *Four Days from Fort Wingate*, Richard French has summoned personalities and facts dealing with the legend of the Adams Diggings and has woven an intriguing tale that will absorb and fascinate his readers. From Sacaton, Arizona, to the myriad rugged canyons of west-central New Mexico, the story unfolds with the skillful blending of past and present events.

If you like adventure, mystery, and tales of the southwestern region of our country, you will find it all in *Four Days from Fort Wingate*.

I.F. BIXLER

ACKNOWLEDGEMENTS

I wish to express my appreciation to certain people who helped me in the research and preparation of this book

My thanks to: Ms. Donna Rimkus of the El Paso Public Library, El Paso, Texas.

Ms. Linda McCleary, Genealogy Librarian of the State of Arizona, Department of Library Archives and Public Records, Phoenix, Arizona.

Ms. Pam Hardenbrook, Editor at The Caxton Printers, Ltd., Caldwell Idaho. Her advice and encouragement helped me a great deal.

Mrs. Linda Rauh of Canton, Oklahoma for her colloraboration in photographic techniques.

Mr. Doug Caldwell, of Colorado's Rocky Mountain National Park, for his editorial assistance.

My deepest appreciation to my wife Lois who was with me throughout this effort.

I shall always be grateful to Mrs. Inez Bixler and her husband Cliff of Denver, Colorado. They became a major part of our story.

Thanks also to Clyde and Henry Lee Summers for their faith and encouragement and for their part in our quest.

Finally, my appreciation to the many people along the way who shared with me their thoughts, their ideas, and their stories.

RICHARD "DICK" FRENCH

INTRODUCTION

The attraction of gold—of treasure—and what it can mean has excited and motivated men and women ever since human history began. There is an old story, a mystery about gold and treasure, that has claimed much more than its fair share of society's attention. In the southwestern U.S. it is known as the legend of the Lost Adams Diggings.

Four Days from Fort Wingate explores and analyzes the Lost Adams tradition. However, before the book is read, there are some facts and statements of old that should be of interest to the reader.

For more than a century, prospectors, adventurers, and writers have given their impressions and opinions of the unusual events surrounding this legend. The following examples offer insight into the story and point out how it captivated members of four generations:

From the *Denver Times,* February 19, 1899, there is this statement by Mr. W.W. Williams of Lake City, Colorado:

> . . . The story which I am about to relate of the Lost Placer Gold mine of New Mexico [the Lost Adams Diggings] does not belong to the mythical class. There were so many participants in its first discovery, and the incidents relating thereto are so well known in California and else-where as to remove the story from the realm of fiction and place it among the remarkable occurrences which have characterized the search for gold in the West . . .

In an excerpt from an article in the *El Paso Herald,* dated February 19, 1916, Mr. W.H. Byerts says:

> This story as handed down by Adams himself tells of what are the richest and largest gold fields known to man and they are in New Mexico, not far from El Paso. The gold mines of Solomon, the Klondike or Africa may not be compared with it.

In his book *Lost Mines of the Great Southwest,* author John D. Mitchell states:

> The search for the famous Adams Diggings has cost the lives of more men than any other lost mine in the great Southwest. Adams searched for years to relocate this fabulously rich placer mine. . . .

The following passages from the 1935 pamphlet *The Adams Diggings Story* by Charles Allen, reveal the following:

> The "Adams Diggings" are the most searched for lost mine in the southwestern portion of the United States.
> . . . It is seventy years since Adams found his famous diggings. He, Jack Davidson and a German, name unknown to the writer, the only members of the original Adams party to return from the diggings, all died long ago, and since then the story of the Adams Diggings has become a legend.

Finally, in his classic book, *Apache Gold and Yaqui Silver,* J. Frank Dobie, states in his Introductory:

> . . . I know a lot more now about Tayopa, the Sierra Madre, and other matters. . . .
> I have an idea that I often know too much for what the average reader regards as good storytelling. I don't think any longer that Tayopa is the greatest lost mine tradition in North America; I think the Lost Adams Diggings is.

Mr. Dobie's explorations and research became known throughout the world in the 1920s and 1930s. Among his many books, *Coronado's Children* and *Apache Gold and Yaqui Silver* bear witness to his expertise on the subjects of lost mines and buried treasures.

In their own way, each of the above writers gained recognition as an authority in the field of mining. If they were alive today, I believe there are two more lines that each might add to his writings about the Lost Adams.

[The richness of this story, its flavor, will never be in finding the gold. It is—just as it has always been—in the quest.]

It is a fact of history that Adams did exist. He did become a legend in his own time. In the years following the Civil War, he told the western pioneers about his incredible adventure involving gold. Today, descendants of those early settlers will tell you that their great grandfather knew Adams and heard the story from him.

As the years passed into decades, and the decades became a century, the Adams revelation deepened into an intriguing mystery that has left a question mark across the Southwest. It is a complicated riddle that thousands of people have tried to unravel.

One of the reasons this tradition has endured is because the story Adams told is very hard to discredit. He talked about his experience, and the Southwest, in the terms of a man who knew what he was talking about. He spoke about gold that was found and then lost, never to be found again. His subject is one that appeals to the adventurer in all of us.

I spent many years researching the Adams revelation; the more I learned about it, the more I came to believe in its validity. The researching and learning process involved many different efforts; and with me in this endeavor was my wife, Lois. Together, we carried our investigation into the libraries of El Paso, Phoenix, Albuquerque, Denver, and a number of other locations in the gathering of information. We took to the highways and traveled to the place where Adams had said it all started, back in 1864. Then, as we began our own search, we went over old trails to some of the landmarks that were written about. Those landmarks were part of the story in Adams' time and they remain an important part of the story today.

Our quest eventually took us over thousands of miles, during which time we dropped down into deep canyons and climbed to the top of high plateaus. In so doing, we found another southwest that only a few have been privileged to see. There were times when inclement weather gave us freezing temperatures and snow drifts. And in July and August, unmoving air in the deep canyons became sultry and the heat nearly unbearable as the temperature climbed to over 100 degrees. Along the way, we found that many other people were involved with the old subject; and we reaped the extra benefit of friendships that will stay with us as long as we live.

Now, I can easily say it was well worth the effort because Lois and I also found an undertaking that really was the kind of thing dreams are made of. For me, one of those dreams was to write the story of the Lost Adams from my own perspective. I have done that in the pages of Four Days from Fort Wingate; and I tried to tell it in a way that would give the reader the same kind of pleasure we experienced as we blended the old with the new.

LIST OF PHOTOGRAPHS

LIST OF ILLUSTRATIONS

A Word From The Author:

Four Days from Fort Wingate was written in first person and it portrays the story of the Lost Adams gold discovery as interpreted by the writer. The author used the nicknames of Terrill and Terry to represent himself and his wife throughout the text.

Something hidden.
Go and find it.
Go and look behind the Ranges—
Something lost behind the Ranges.
Lost and waiting for you.
Go.

KIPLING, "The Explorer" (1903)

FOUR DAYS
FROM
FORT WINGATE

1

THE LEGEND

In the month of August in the year 1864, at a place in Arizona Territory called Sacaton, a party of twenty-three men formed an alliance; their objective, a quest for *gold.*

The quest—a remarkable adventure for a few, a fatal step in harm's way for others—produced one of the most puzzling mysteries of the developing West. It went on to become one of America's more enduring and profoundly interesting legends.

Down through the years, what had begun as a frontier story became the subject of letters, newspaper and magazine articles, books, and (more recently) motion picture productions. Long before the printed versions occurred, this narrative about a great gold discovery reached a high level of fascination for the pioneers as it traveled by word of mouth across the frontier.

Sacaton, where the story began, is one of several Pima Indian villages situated near the Gila (pronounced Hee-la) River only a few miles south of present-day Phoenix, Arizona. This hot and desolate location, where summer temperatures often range between 100 and 110 degrees, has been home to the Pimas for centuries.

From the days of early Spanish explorations, the Pimas have been at peace with other cultures who happened to come their way. With much of western civilization during the 1860s limited to friendly Indian settlements and widely spaced forts, the Pima villages became a meeting place and point of supply for travelers going from El Paso and Tucson to Yuma and places farther west in California.

Accounts of the past offer certain facts about a chain of incidents that took place in Sacaton in 1864. A large party of men, twenty-one being the most often-called number, were temporarily camped there. They claimed to be miners on their way to the gold fields in California. They had gold pans and other gold hunting tools, and made a number of prospecting trips into the nearby hills.

Large groups of men traveling together were not uncommon in those days. They often banded together in the eastern states for protection, among other reasons, during their continental passage.

Of the twenty-one men in the mining party, only three played important roles in the creation of the legend. There was a German who spoke only broken English, and then only in answer to questions. He was a private, reserved man in his early fifties. The others called him Dutch or simply the German.

The second man was tall, slender, and in his mid-sixties. He was always the first one up in the morning, whistling and making coffee. His name was Davidson. He had a vibrant personality and even with the usual complaints about the coffee, he was well liked by all.

Then, there was John Brewer. He was a cautious, observant man, constantly aware of what was going on around him. John had thrown in with the party of miners at Santa Fe. For his thirty-nine years, he had traveled a good deal, and much of his traveling had taken place in the West. John Brewer had learned well, and he had the respect of the others when it came to dealing with the frontier and the pioneer people who lived there.

Apart from the mining party itself, another traveler was camped a few miles out from Sacaton. Adams, for whom the legend became known, stood looking at his burning wagons. In an early-morning raid, renegade Indians had managed to put an end to his freighting business. He had saved his saddle horse and used it in retrieving his wagon team, which had been run off by the raiders as a diversion. Returning, he found his wagons on fire. Devastated at that moment, he turned toward Sacaton, thinking someone there might buy his horses.

According to the old story, Adams was a comparatively young man in 1864, probably in his late thirties. An adventurous type, Adams had come west from the state of New York.

In Sacaton itself, there was a bright-eyed young man who had become friendly with the miners. He was smart, well liked by all, and had seen much more of the world than most of his peers in Sacaton. The youth was of mixed blood, half Mexican and half Pima Indian. In contrast to the others in the story, he was a part of the West. With a Mexican father and a Pima mother, he was as much a part of that exciting land as the ponderosa pine or the redding sky of a desert sunset.

When he was just a child, Apaches had raided his home and killed his parents. The Apache band took him and his brother as slaves. The two boys lived with their abductors for many years. Then, in an argument, the Apaches killed his brother.

In 1864, the half-breed was a developing young man in his late teens or early twenties, who had fled his captors seeking a better way of life. Because of this, he had little more than the clothes on his back when he became acquainted with the mining men. Like any other young man of that day, he wanted his own horse, a sidearm, and the necessities that made life more complete. He was, therefore, a candidate for gainful employment.

The young Pima-Mexican had seen something once; something rare. Only two years before, he had been on an expedition with the Apaches when they raided Pueblo Indians in western New Mexico. At one of the raiders' campsites, he had seen gold, pieces of it larger than acorns. For its size, he could not believe how heavy it was—and that color, bright yellow!

Just beneath two rounded peaks was a seam in a hidden canyon wall; this heavy, yellow material was embedded in the glassy rocks that were a part of the seam. The Apaches told him to forget about the yellow rock. They said that the use of it was determined by tribal leaders. What they had told him then, however, mattered little to him now.

Because of his heritage, the Pima-Mexican had an appreciation for artistic works made of silver and turquoise, but he had never seen gold used in this manner. Neither did he have any knowledge of its value. This is why, when the miners displayed a great enthusiasm over some tiny nuggets they found nearby, the young half-breed laughed. The miners looked at him with scorn.

John Brewer, seeing that the youth was genuinely amused, thought about the boy's strange reaction for a moment, then produced two coins made of gold. The mining men saw the amused expression change to real interest and then to something bordering on amazement.

The half-breed looked at Brewer, his dark brown eyes flashing with excitement as he exclaimed, "Listen, compadre! I know a place where canyon walls cry tears of this every day! And those tears are larger than your coins!"

At that, everyone laughed—except the young half-breed and John Brewer. Brewer could see something in those dark eyes. The youth was quite serious.

After the laughter died down, and after repeated assurances by the Pima-Mexican, the miners showed interest in his story. They pressed him for information about the location of this fabulous canyon.

He pointed to the northeast and told them it was much closer than the California gold fields they were bound for.

"I can take you there!"

For one reason or another, the miners came to believe him. It may have been something as simple as the straightforward and honest way in which he told them about the place—a canyon in Apacheria—where gold was plentiful. Possibly, the Pima-Mexican had some nuggets by way of proof. Large nuggets would have made it hard to discount such a story. At any rate they did believe him, and struck a deal with him to become their guide and lead them to this remarkable valley of gold.

The young half-breed had the job and with it came the means to get himself a horse, a saddle, a gun, and, according to tradition, some of the gold. The bargain also called for his execution in the event he failed to deliver what he so ardently promised.

The miners badly needed horses. It was a different world then. There were no highways, no cars, no trucks or buses. No jets streaked across the sky to haul a commuting America from coast to coast. The only real means of getting anywhere was by horse and a party like this one also needed pack animals to carry supplies.

Fate, almost as though by some intricate design, brought Adams and his wagon teams into the Pima village at just the right moment. The badly needed horses must have been a delightful sight to the miners. Soon they were talking to Adams, telling him about the young Pima and his captivating story of gold.

At length, an agreement was reached and an alliance was formed. For the next several days, the men gathered supplies and worked on equipment while they made preparations for their undertaking. There was much activity in Sacaton.

Looking back to that long ago setting, it does appear that these people were used to bring about one of those fascinating pages in America's history.

The first part of their effort took them east along the Gila River to its confluence with the San Carlos River. From here, they turned north and followed the San Carlos until it took a turn to the east. It is generally believed that the mining party left the San Carlos River then and traveled northward to two other stream crossings: the Black River first and then the White River.

For the next two days, they followed the White River and its east fork up into the White Mountains. The headwaters of the East Fork are formed there in the rugged terrain between Mt. Ord and Mt. Baldy.

One of the facts coming down to us from Adams, states that from a mountain lookout the miners observed several mountain ranges. Among those were the San Francisco Mountains, near modern Flagstaff, and other peaks lying to the north, northeast, and east. Adams was certain this lookout was located either on Mt. Ord, or on one of the mountaintops nearby.

He said that after their expedition had climbed up to a high point among the peaks, their guide pointed out two, close-setting, mountain points. The guide told his party, "The canyon *del oro* (canyon of the gold) is not far from those peaks."

Adams is further quoted as saying the two distant points looked at least one hundred miles away and the direction to the two points was northeast. He also recalled that the expedition maintained a general course setting of northeast from its beginning.

That being the case, the lookout producing the view of the ranges just described is, no doubt, located among the higher crests of the White Mountains. It is also logical to conclude that the lookout was near the halfway mark of their journey, and that the remaining half was simply a continuation of the now precedented northeasterly course.

At the time, Adams thought the two peaks that had been pointed out by the guide as being near the gold would provide a reference point, a beacon they would be working toward for the next few days. As Adams would subsequently discover, however, this was not to be the case.

One of the most important sources for the many facts that make up this legend is a publication called *The Adams Diggings Story,* written by Charles Allen and published in 1935 by the Hughes-Buie Company, El Paso, Texas. Many years after the original quest for gold took place, Allen became a long-time friend and prospecting partner of Captain C. A. Shaw, a financial backer and prospecting partner of Adams.

According to Allen, in relaying Adams' words, from the beginning, until nearing the end of their endeavor, the party traveled on *long established Indian trails.*[1] This statement, like the one stating that they had held a general northeasterly course, is quite important. If indeed they did cross the vast Southwest, as Adams claimed, by using existing Indian trails, then a question presents itself: Where would those trails normally take the travelers who used them?

Much of the area of the White Mountains of eastern Arizona was developed by various Apache bands. Their civilization had long since made trails along streams such as the White River, but the Indians had not done as much with the country to the east, into New Mexico.

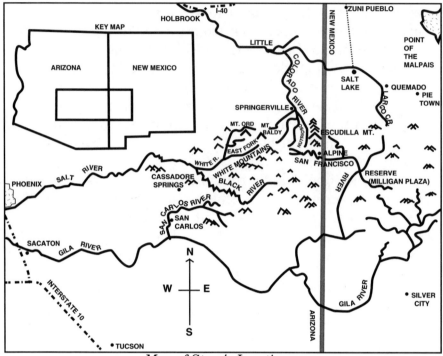

Map of Story's Locations.

Although the Apache often traveled this region, they did not develop many long-lasting interests there. The Pueblo Indian settlements were far apart as were the Navajo concentrations.

Trails crossing the arid deserts were few, and most were much longer than those in the White Mountains. Both Navajos and Apaches created improved routes across western New Mexico, a result of their nomadic life styles. For the white man, little civilization existed. Some 1864 maps show portions of western New Mexico as unexplored. It was *Apacheria* and traveling through it was a dangerous gamble for anyone—except the Apaches.

Thus, when the young Pima-Mexican led his party of twenty-three armed miners into that wild, primitive part of Apacheria, it was something of a show of force.

The northeasterly course was, naturally, a general term. Sometimes the trails they followed, because of the physical nature of the terrain, simply veered more to the north or to the east. One such occasion faced the men when they left the high country.

Indian trails led away from the White Mountains in many directions, and some controversy has developed regarding which of those trails the mining party followed. Most accounts agree in substance, that the primary direction taken in this instance was north.

Going east and only a few degrees north would put one on a collision course with Escudilla (es-ka-dia), a massive mountain that overlooked a vast area and rose to an elevation of almost 11,000 feet. The fact that the party had to circumvent this obstacle, going either north or south of it, created two scenarios of thought. Writers and seekers of the Adams' treasure have given credibility to both.

A. M. Tenney, Jr., in articles that were published by the *El Paso Herald* in 1927 and 1928 and later reprinted by the *Frontier Times* magazine, told of meeting a returning John Brewer. The meeting, which occurred in the late 1880s, was held at Tenney's father's farm near the present site of Springerville, Arizona.[2]

Brewer's account will be discussed later in this narrative; for now, we shall take only a portion of his story—that part dealing with the route that was taken by the original expedition as they departed the region of Mt. Ord. They were still high in the mountains, as Brewer recalled.

> Before leaving the timber we took note of our surroundings. Directly in front of us and on the route we were to take we could see a vast area of open country with high lava hills and rough canyons which we would have to cross.

> To the right and about thirty miles distant we could
> see a round, timber-covered mountain (Escudilla moun-
> tains). Directly in front of us and about fifteen miles dis-
> tant we were able to trace the course of the Little
> Colorado river as it made its way out of the mountains
> toward the north.3

John Brewer's account leaves no room for argument
when it comes to the course taken by the party in relation to the Escudilla Mountain Range. They traveled
from the southwest to the northeast with the vast
Escudilla Mountain to their right.

Other writers confirmed this line of reasoning.
Charles Allen's previously mentioned pamphlet, *The
Adams Diggings Story* (which we will refer to from this
point on as the Allen Account) is one of these confirma-
tions. In it, Adams remembered the way the mining
party moved out of the high country, and out of the timber of the White Mountains.

He said, essentially, that they traveled downhill for
two days as they made their departure from the higher
elevations of the White Mountains. He spoke of moving
toward the east for several miles; then, as they followed
a small stream, the long column of riders went north.
Adams thought this stream was the Nutrioso, but he
was not sure.[4] It could have been any number of streams
that flow north toward what is now Springerville,
Arizona. Just which one it was is not known, but Adams
said they spent their second night from Mt. Ord, camped
on its banks.

These movements, described by Charles Allen, as
first told by Adams, would have undoubtedly placed
Escudilla Mountain east of the mining party. That indi-
cates, quite logically, that the trail they were on would
have to skirt the big mountain on its north side if their
ultimate destination was northeast of the White
Mountains.

Escudilla Mountain, Point of Mystery

Further collaboration of this view is given by Ben W. Kemp and J. C. Dykes in their book titled *Cow Dust and Saddle Leather.* This book is a fine collection of experiences and events that were an important part of our developing western culture. One of the chapters in this book is called "The Adams Story." In this chapter, the writers tell about the Kemp family's connection with the adventurous Mr. Adams.

In this instance, Adams tells how the original expedition had taken a course away from the Pima villages, going in a northeasterly direction. After several days on the trial, they made camp at a point only *two miles* east of what is now the site of Springerville.[5] That location is only a few miles north-northwest of the northern slopes of Escudilla Mountain. It is also a fact that Nutrioso Creek flows northward, out of the White Mountains, through a canyon just *two miles* east of Springerville.

In discussing these three sources—and there were others with the view that the mining party had rounded Escudilla Mountain to the north—it is my purpose to show a point beyond which the old original trail became obscured in ambiguity, lost to everyone who attempted to follow the route described by Adams. Landmarks that were relatively easy to follow appear to have come to a halt near Escudilla Mountain.

The original party went on and found a fantastic gold deposit. That party was attacked and only a few, including Adams, survived. The indecisive search patterns by Adams and others in later years provide evidence that the trail to the gold went cold quickly, near Escudilla Mountain.

Adams also mentioned a second set of landmarks to the frontiersmen. Just as impressive as the first, the second group of landmarks occurred within two days' ride of the gold. Locating the second set of landmarks has confounded searchers for more than a hundred years.

A number of accounts state that Adams returned many times to Milligan Plaza, now called Reserve. It is known that he also visited Horse Springs and Magdalena, all New Mexico locations. He thought the San Francisco River near Milligan Plaza was familiar. There were landmarks in that vicinity that he believed were passed on the first trip.

If so, it would seem only logical for the party to go east and a little south of the Mt. Ord-Mt. Baldy region to the area now known as Alpine, Arizona. The group could then have followed the San Francisco River east, right to the place that later became Milligan Plaza. However, if the party had followed this route, they would have passed south of Escudilla Mountain, not north.

Confusing? Yes, and it was even more so for Adams when he made his many efforts to reclaim the gold he had once seen.

Which way *did* the original mining party go? This is one of the questions that remains unanswered to the present day. There are other questions as well, and together they comprise the puzzling ingredients that make up the mystery of the Lost Adams.

In *Cow Dust and Saddle Leather,* Adams, in Ben Kemp's words, tells us that for two days after they left the camp near the Springerville site, he was in a dazed, confused state. It could be, as Ben Kemp suggested, that Adams might have tapped the whiskey keg too much.[6]

In the previously mentioned Tenney version, Brewer tells us his recollection of that part of the trip. The miners were leaving the cover of the mountains. They were edgy, worried, and concerned about the Indian threat.[7] Whatever the distraction, it seems that both survivors of that first expedition, lost the trail forever in the Escudilla Mountain-Springerville site area.

To me, it seems quite possible that whatever was befuddling one of these survivors may very well not have been the cause of the other's confusion. In the Tenney article, there is no mention of John Brewer ever taking his search into the Reserve area or the San Francisco River valley. It is a fact of the story, however, that an extended period of time passed between the original party's excursion into that primitive wilderness and the return of these two survivors.

Twelve to fifteen years or longer, as was the case with Brewer, could make a difference in a man's memory. This is especially true of a person like Adams whose experience in mountain travel was limited and whose sense of direction was notably poor. It must be remembered that the first party covered a great deal of terrain, terrain that changed, yet at the same time also looked much like that passed the previous day.

Ultimately, at the end of their long trail, they found gold in such quantities as to delight the soul of the most unimpressionable human being. Then they witnessed

those other extremes: *terror, despair,* and *death!* Among
other things, their adventure found the deep, wide spec-
trum of raw human emotion. Few of our species have
known such a pendulum swing.

Although the trail seems lost near Escudilla
Mountain, it did not stop there. According to some
accounts, the expedition continued for three more days,
while others say six. Through the words of those early
writers, Adams and Brewer reveal something about that
stark, rugged part of their trip.

After leaving the Springerville area campsite, the
miners had to make a dry camp, one where water was
not available. This was probably on one of those high
plateaus that are common to the country northeast of
Springerville. That part of western New Mexico is a
combination of plateaus, deserts, and cedar-covered
hills. Lava flows are prevalent over much of it, as indicated by widespread lava rock.

We know they traveled a course between due east
and due north. The mining party entered a vast, uncom-
promising region of ten thousand square miles, a part of
which J. Frank Dobie once described as being "the loneli-
est and eeriest point of habitation north of the Andes in
the Western hemisphere."[8] The area is today framed by
the Rio Grande River on the east, Interstate Highway 40
on the north, on the west the Arizona state line, and the
Gila National Forest on the south. Within that ten thousand square miles people have always been few in number; that fact remains true today.

The party rode on, penetrating deep into this land
the Apaches called their own. One afternoon they went
downhill for several hours, reaching a stream of clear,
cool water. That water flowed to the northwest along a
valley lined with giant cottonwood trees.

On another occasion, they camped at a spring surrounded by ash trees. Still another time, their guide
took them into a basin where they bathed in a warm

water spring. The riders rode up long grades, down into deep canyons, and through picturesque mountain cuts. They crossed malpais-studded prairies where they saw the weathering evidence of ancient volcanic activity.

No matter where they rode, it was August and hot throughout much of each day. It was also the monsoon season, and that meant afternoon thunderstorms. The view from their saddles would have shown them distant showers scattered over a mixture of prairies and hills covered with cedar and pinon trees. At times, when thunderheads moved across their path, electrical storms and downpours forced them out of their saddles to seek whatever shelter they could find. Today, we drive along our highways, pass through these thunderstorms and think nothing of it. If the temperature drops, we just cut back on the air conditioner and remain dry and comfortable. Soon, perhaps ten or fifteen minutes, the storm is behind us and forgotten.

Looking back now to the time when I first became interested in the Adams story, I remember how frustrating it was to read those old texts, trying to find some pattern, some organization, a key that would tell me: *go and dig there.* However, as one-by-one I came into possession of the various versions of the story I discovered that the legend only held more questions and fewer answers. Eventually, I realized that even though there were many facts concerning the route taken by the Pima-Mexican guide, there was no way anyone could place those facts, and the events they represented, in the sequence in which they originally occurred. Adams himself had been unable to do it. Writers of the past tried to do so with information they possessed at the time. Readers and searchers alike believed them, and that produced something of a distortion of truth. Now, in the more than 130 years of the story's life, we can see how this has added to the mystery.

It is time now to pick up the riders as they move toward their destination and that second set of landmarks.

Recall that the miners had been on the trail, away from the Springerville area camp, for a number of days. As stated before, the accounts do not agree on the number, but as nearly as this writer can tell, the expedition was probably in its third day from that Springerville camp when it came to a wide path, or what some accounts called a *wagon road.*

The guide informed his company that they should take careful notice of this *wagon road,* because they would have to return to it in order to obtain supplies from a military post that was located at the end of the road. There was no other source for supplies anywhere near them. By that point in time, the value of new provisions was certainly becoming important. The men had been in the saddle for at least twelve days. Even though the expedition had been able to kill game for meat along the way, other staple items such as coffee, salt, sugar, etc. were running short.

They would have to replenish their supplies somewhere. Accordingly, it is necessary to have some knowledge of old fort locations of that era. Only a few degrees variance from true northeast of Mt. Ord, about 140 miles or so, was Old Fort Wingate. This was the original site of the fort bearing the name Wingate, and it was located near the modern city of Grants, New Mexico. Almost directly north of Mt. Ord, at nearly the same distance, was Fort Canby in northeastern Arizona.

At the time the mining expedition took place, Fort Defiance, also in northeastern Arizona, had been abandoned and its former jurisdiction had become the responsibility of Fort Canby. Fort Defiance was reestablished in 1868 as the Navajo Indian Agency. About halfway between Fort Canby and Fort Wingate was Fort

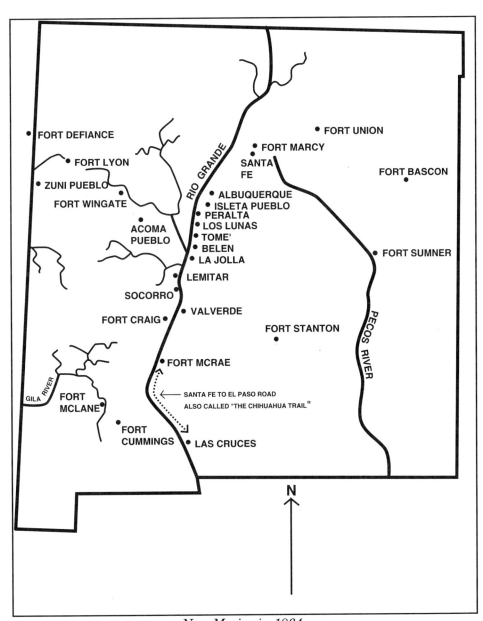

New Mexico in 1864.

Lyon, however, in 1864, Fort Lyon was only a mail station, and supplies were not available there.

The only other fort in existence at that time in this general area—actually, in the entire west-central and northwestern portions of New Mexico—was Fort Craig. It does not appear likely, however, that Fort Craig would have been the source of their provisions. For one thing, Fort Craig was a little south of a line running east from Mt. Ord, and was located on the Rio Grande River.

Nothing in any of the accounts suggests Fort Craig as a source of supplies, or mentions the Rio Grande. On the other hand, Old Fort Wingate has been mentioned so many times as the probable supply point that it appears certain to have been just that.

With the crossing of the old trail, or wagon road, the old accounts offer much the same information, and to some degree, the same order of events. The mining party moved on and soon entered a wide arroyo or dry wash, and for the next few hours moved along this wash. Then the gold seekers left the old, well-beaten Indian trail and took a dim, less-traveled track that led them off in a more northerly direction

They apparently rode for a few miles more over lower terrain, before the new trail began climbing. After a while, the miners found themselves on a large tableland. From that tableland, or mesa, they could look back and see most of the desert area they had ridden through that day. Here, on this elevated mesa, they came across an area with many vines and what appeared to be old, eroded irrigation ditches. Whether they were pumpkin vines, or wild gourds is not clear, but Adams named the place *Pumpkin Patch,* and the name has endured. By this time, the sun was low in the west, and the men decided the patch would be a good place in which to spend the night.

Early the next morning, the party left the *Pumpkin Patch* and rode up to a reddish-colored bluff. The bluff was described as a solid rock wall sixty to seventy feet high. It continued for an extensive distance both to the right and to the left.

Some of the riders wondered how they were going to get around it. Their guide, however, had been there before, and directed them to a crack in the escarpment, which turned out to be an opening that could be seen only at close range.

In later years, Adams referred to this as the *Little Door*. He said that, one at a time, the riders entered the passageway and rode through the bluff for about 150 yards. The passage was narrow all the way, so close, in fact, that he could touch the walls occasionally by extending his arms outward as he rode along.

When they emerged from this crevasse, they were in a rough, broad canyon that supported some timber and contained much exposed rock and large boulders. They traveled most of that day going upstream in this little valley. Between three and four in the afternoon, the party reached the upper end of the canyon.

In a little steeper climb, the dim trail topped out of the canyon's head onto another mesa. This one was level and apparently quite high. Most of the surrounding region could be observed from there.

From this high mesa the young guide once more pointed out what he said were the two mountain points they had seen from the White Mountains. This time, they were only a matter of hours away. That gave cause for real excitement among the members of the expedition because it meant that at last, they were nearing the end of this great effort. Soon they would be in El Dorado, mining the treasure, possessing the *gold*.

The Pima-Mexican told his happy charges that they had the better part of another day's ride to reach their destination. Again he pointed east and said the gold was in a canyon near the two mountains that were clearly visible. As they studied the route ahead, the twenty-two

men were glad they had their guide. The country to the
east was a literal maze of canyons. Only the two mountains rose out of that maze, and the effect was stunning.

Their dark complexioned guide then told the miners
about the ledge along the canyon wall that held the gold;
about the rough country that the canyon was in, and
about the creek where the sand was rich with gold dust.
Once more he told them about the glassy rock and how
it contained threads and chunks of the bright yellow
metal.

As they gathered in around him, every man heard
every word. Those words were exciting, thrilling, and
full of promise, and they provided the mining partners
with that rare anticipation known only to those who
have dared to dream on such a scale.

Only a few hours of daylight remained as the guide
led the long column of riders down, off the high mesa,
into a deep canyon. When they reached the floor of the
canyon, they found a spring with running water, which
they followed for a short distance to a small acre-sized
meadow. This is where the guide told them to make
camp for the night.

In some of the accounts, Adams describes this
canyon as having high, perpendicular walls. He said
that the trail down into the canyon was steep, with a
number of switchbacks that formed a zigzag pattern
among the rocks, trees, and drop-offs.

However, other versions, of which the Allen Account
is one, tell a different story. According to Allen, the miners did descend into a long, narrow valley, but they got
there by means of a gentle, sloping trail.[9] The truth is
probably to be found somewhere between these two versions. As a result of the way in which time affects human
memory, I feel that both versions may be exaggerated.

While the miners were dismounting in the meadow
their guide mentioned, almost as though he was looking
for something to say, "There is a little gold in the creek

here." Since it was still about an hour before sundown, two of the miners broke out their gold pans to check out that low-key statement.

Adams, as he later related this part of his adventure, told of an astonished group of men. What their young guide had just called a little gold turned out to be as much as two ounces of gold per pan load of gravel. They checked it out, all right, and could not believe their eyes. Making camp, fixing something to eat, and everything else was forgotten in favor of washing the gravel. That night, they worked the gravel until they could no longer see.

The young half-breed reportedly told them several times that this was not the place to which he was leading them. He said there was much more gold only one more day's ride toward the two peaks, however, no one would listen. They had their strike already.

By noon the following day, the miners had prospected the canyon both upstream and downstream from camp, and there was gold, gold, gold!

Even before noon of that extraordinary day Adams had panned out enough gold to more than pay for his lost freight wagons. It was the happiest day of his life. All of the miners were simply overwhelmed with what they had found. They knew the discovery was a great one, and in only a matter of days they would be rich.

According to the legend, the young guide was paid well: a saddle horse and saddle, a pack horse, the pistol and holster that he had his heart set on, and some of the first day's take of the gold. He left the party the second night, but not before issuing a warning.

He told the group that they should not stay long in the canyon. It was the campsite of roving Apaches, and the mining party might be in danger if they were caught there. However, now that they had found their dream, the prospectors were not easily discouraged.

A few days after the Pima-Mexican's departure, a band of Indians did enter the canyon and set up camp. Adams said the people were not hostile to the mining party. In fact, just the opposite occurred.

Another of the accounts I have used in the assembling of this information is that of W. H. Byerts and his story entitled *Lost Adams Diggings*. This article first appeared in the *El Paso Herald* of February 19, 1916.

On the point regarding the Indians that were encamped near the Adams party, Byerts, quoting Adams directly, wrote about a peaceful band of Indians who were friendly with the miners. Right from the beginning, the Indian children of the band roamed between the two camps. Then, overnight, a change came about. Without any communication at all, the Indians left.[10]

This odd and unexpected switch in the behavior of their Indian neighbors seemed to put the miners on edge. As a result, Adams said that the men then became a little more cautious and aware of what was going on around them.

The gold miners continued to mine their gold. They made a decision to pool the dust and nuggets, and divide it at a later date. Reportedly, all participated, with the exception of the German, who wanted to work his diggings separately and keep his gold production to himself.

A period of time passed. Supplies were about to run out. A meeting was called and it was decided that some of the men would make a trip back to the wagon road and then on to the fort for the provisions. The party included one man who professed some knowledge of the country. He said he recognized the wagon road and estimated the distance to the fort from the gold strike at about four days' travel, one way. Some writers have concluded that this was John Brewer.

By that time, the German had become nervous about staying in the canyon. He was afraid of Indians, and the guide's warning had played on that fear until he found it hard to concentrate on his work. He wanted to go out with the provisions party, at least to the wagon road, from which point he would follow the back trail to Arizona alone. He did that, and with him went better than sixty pounds of gold that he had mined from a place about the size of a wagon bed and only two feet deep—according to Adams—according to Charles Allen.

The German made it back to Sacaton and then to Yuma where he cashed in his gold to a storekeeper. Some time later, he bought cattle and started a ranch near Prescott, Arizona. According to the Allen Account, the German was killed on his cattle ranch in 1867.[11] Another story, however, claims he cashed in his gold and went back to the east coast, where he bought a steamship ticket for Europe. He went to his native Germany and never returned to the New World.[12]

Meanwhile, those who stayed in the canyon began construction of a log cabin to house them through the winter. Along one wall, they constructed a rock fireplace. As the story goes, they selected one large rock with a deep recess and placed it under the hearth. Then, being careful to pick just what was needed, they found another rock, this one broad, flat, and several inches thick.

This second rock was to serve two purposes. It would be the hearthstone that would be covered with sand and upon which the evening fires would be built. It would also be the door to the vault, a heavy door that would take two men to move it. This was security for the gold that would be deposited in the recessed cavity of the lower rock.

And so it went, day after day, each man working long, hard hours. At the end of the day, they made their deposits in this incredible vault.

Nine days after the provisions party left, Adams became concerned about their safety. He and the man named Davidson decided to climb out of the canyon, up

to the high tableland, in the hope of seeing the returning men. That morning, they rose before sunrise, wanting to get an early start.

The pair reached the place where the guide had
pointed out the two mountains, but there was still no
sign of the provisions party. They crossed the high mesa
and right where the trail began its descent into the long
canyon—they found them!

Adams said it was a horrifying sight. Bodies were
scattered along the trail for two hundred feet, some
beheaded. He said it looked to him and Davidson as
though it had happened within the last twenty-four
hours, probably near sundown the night before.

Apparently the assailants had waited for the supply
party on the edge of the mesa and from that high ground
had launched an ambush. The men returning with the
provisions never had a chance. It was a devastating
attack. In the frenzy of battle, the Indians had even
killed one of the horses.

Working as quickly as they could, Adams and
Davidson placed their comrades' bodies in a rock wall
cavity. They covered them with packsaddles and rocks in
an attempt to protect them from animal predators.

The ambushers had taken the surviving horses and
most of the supplies, but Adams noticed a steel crosscut
saw that had been left behind. It had been purchased for
the purpose of cutting boards out of logs to make sluice
boxes; at this turn of events, it had suddenly become
useless and was left where it lay. The time was about
nine o'clock as the two men rode hurriedly across the
mesa and started back down the trail to warn the others.

Then, just as though fate had fired one shot from a
double-barreled shotgun, suddenly, the second concus-
sion went off! Adams and Davidson heard war whoops
and screams—*soul-wrenching screams!* In another surprise assault, a large party of Indians had descended

upon the camp and was in the process of running down and killing the remaining miners. Adams said the fear that gripped him was complete. Still, he and Davidson had the presence of mind to take the necessary steps for self-preservation.

The two men, being careful not to leave tracks, worked their way back up on top of the high mesa. They knew tracks would bring swift pursuit, so they dismounted, hid the saddles, and turned their horses loose. After that, they fled across the mesa on foot, walking on rock surfaces wherever they could, finally taking refuge in a brushy cedar thicket at the far end of the plateau.

Adams wondered how he and Davidson had missed coming face-to-face with the Indians. He had thought there was only one way in and out of the canyon, that being over the trail the two of them had used that morning. Later, after giving the matter some consideration, he decided that after hitting the provisions party, the attackers had slipped by the miners' camp after the miners had turned in for the night. Then with the benefit of a good night's rest, the raiders attacked the gold mining camp.

In making the early climb out of the canyon that fateful morning, Adams and Davidson had managed to beat the angel of death by only a matter of hours.

The two survivors spent the rest of that day in hiding. They were simply too afraid to venture out of their hideaway in the daylight. Adams looked out of his concealment just as the sun was setting, seeing once more, the two peaks the Pima-Mexican had pointed out.

Reflecting back on that moment in later years, he said the two mountains looked to him like big stacks of hay in the evening sunlight. He never forgot that impression. Adams also remembered thinking that if the mining party had gone on to the place the guide had wanted to take them, this tragedy might have been avoided.

It was well after dark when the two survivors slipped cautiously down the trail toward the canyon. From a high point, they looked down on what had been the cabin site. The raiding Indians had turned it into a giant bonfire and were dancing wildly around the inferno.

Nineteen men dead, Adams thought to himself; the thought choked his soul with remorse. Then he thought about the gold under that hearthstone and how the Indians would probably never know it was there. He found little consolation in such thinking, however.

What he and Davidson did not know then, and were never to find out, was that far below them in the deep darkness of that hideous night—there was another survivor.

John Brewer had also escaped and was lying terrified under a cedar growth against a rock wall. In the next few days, his life began anew as he found his way to the Rio Grande River.

The gory victory dancing continued late into the night. Decapitated heads of the miners were mounted at the tops of poles and held high above the dancers. Finally, about two o'clock in the morning, the Indians pulled out and made their way down the canyon to their own camp.

Adams claimed that there was no way to reach the gold. The green logs were still smoldering and had collapsed inward on the hearth when he and Davidson made their way to the deserted camp. What the Indians had not plundered, the darkness concealed. As a result, they salvaged nothing.

The gold used to buy the supplies at the fort, the small amount paid to the guide, the sixty-plus pounds taken out by the German, and two nuggets Adams had in his pocket when he escaped comprised all the gold that had been removed from the canyon. That was low payment indeed for the lives of eighteen men.

The two survivors, thankful for their good fortune, quickly left the area. It is generally thought that they went in a westerly direction and covered as much country as they could before the approach of dawn drove them into hiding once more. This time, their refuge was in a grove of aspen trees. When they decided it was safe to leave the aspens, they resumed their journey for about ten days, traveling mostly at night, aiming for Arizona. Here again, the truth about what happened has been lost to us, obscured by those who told the story and by those who wrote it down.

There is an account of the pair having been picked up by a detachment of troops traveling from Old Fort Wingate to Fort Tularosa, a post that was not built until 1872. Another version states they found their way to Fort Apache in Arizona. However, as with Fort Tularosa, Fort Apache was still many years away in 1864.

Yet another story tells us that the two men were found about twenty-five miles northwest of Silver City, New Mexico, by a cavalry unit out of Fort West. Fort West was established in 1863, but had been abandoned in January 1864, eight months before the Adams expedition took place. Another old tradition claims the two survivors were picked up by troopers from Old Fort Wingate and taken there.

After Adams and Davidson had spent a week recuperating at Fort Wingate, the post commander insisted that they lead a burial detail back to the scene of the massacres. It would seem only logical that, if this were true and a burial party did indeed go out from Fort Wingate, there would be little mystery regarding the location of the Lost Adams gold.

At any rate, Adams and Davidson did make it out and to my thinking, the Allen Account found in Chapter 2, offers the best explanation of their escape.

In any event, following their escape, Adams went to his Los Angeles home where he was reported to have

spent the next twelve to fifteen years raising his children. Not until the U.S. Army curtailed the menacing
Apache and Navajo raiders did he consider returning to
search for the gold.

It has been written that Davidson did not live long
after he and Adams were found, but the truth is, he lived
long enough to be the originator of some aspects of the
story.

When Adams finally did return, he made a number
of trips trying to relocate the fabulous gold deposit he
had once been privileged to see. He is said to have taken
large parties of men into the San Francisco River area,
near what is now Reserve. He took another group into
northeastern Arizona, but each effort ended in failure.
He could not find the old landmarks that would have
put him back on the right track again.

Many became disgusted with him. Some wanted to
take his life because of his inability to find anything definite. There were also those who hunted with him for
years. All who knew Adams well said that he was honest and that the story he told was true.

Byerts, who was well acquainted with several men
who had worked with Adams, spoke highly of the man.

> No man ever talked to Adams but felt that Adams was a
> man of strong character and talked only the truth. He
> would give the facts in such a positive and candid way
> that no one doubted his sincerity for a moment.13

This was only one statement among many in support of Adams. Over the years before his death, he
became a living legend, he and his incredible story of
what has been described as the greatest gold discovery
of all time. We can only imagine the disappointment he
must have felt through all those years, to remember so
well that unusual canyon, only to fail in his efforts to
locate it again.

So there it is, a story of gold, of adventure, an appealing mystery, and finally a story of death. The telling about it went forth and triggered a great legend. It is a tale that continues to stir the blood of those who dream, even now, more than 130 years after the fact.

Many still search for that old cabin site and the weathering fireplace with its waiting hearth. They search . . . and they wonder.

2

THE SURVIVORS

In any conflict, there are the victorious and the defeated. In this case, the victorious rode away unscathed, untouched, and they did so because of offensive strategies: ambush and surprise assault.

In every conflict, the list of survivors must include the victors. Without that inclusion, there can be no true accounting of survivors.

The victors in this case were Indians. Early writers of the legend contend they were Apaches. Some of the old accounts specifically name the Apache chief Nana and his band of warriors. The incident took place in what was called Apacheria, a region somewhat under threat from roving Apache bands. Thus, it is logical to assume that the perpetrators probably were Apaches.

The area in question, however, was also the home of several normally peaceful Pueblo Indian tribes. There were also widely scattered Navajo branches over much of Apacheria. Consequently, we have a situation when logical assumption might not necessarily render the truth.

While the strike force may never be identified, the thoroughness with which they carried out their tactics is obvious. It is also quite obvious that the attacks were the result of a plan. A plan implies premeditation, and premeditation comes from motivation. The question, why did it happen, was not so thoroughly examined in the old accounts. One has to wonder whether it was the gold or was it the result of friction over something that occurred between the Indians and the miners?

If it was the gold, were the Indians motivated out of greed or fear: Did they covet the metal, or were they intimidated by it?

There was a time, during the latter half of the nineteenth century, when Indians bought supplies from the various trading posts and forts and paid for those supplies with raw gold. Although members of many tribes indulged in such transactions, the exchange of gold for commodities never reached a level above what we today would call small commercial trading. The mining of gold by Indians in Apacheria, on a large scale simply never took place. It is because of this fact that we know the Indians, whoever they were, that attacked the Adams party, left the gold alone. This would seem to indicate that it was fear rather than greed that provided the motivation. It is difficult to understand such an attitude about gold when the metal was widely distributed in placers and lodes, from New Mexico and Colorado through Arizona and Nevada to California.

The native inhabitants chose not to develop their gold when most of the other peoples of the earth, including the Indians of Mexico and South America, did the opposite. It makes one wonder if perhaps there may have been a time—before the Spaniards—when the Native American inhabitants of the Southwest thought differently about their gold?

The Survivors of the Alliance

A survivor is one who remains in existence. He outlasts and outlives those who go down in death.

From the massacres at the canyon of gold, there were five survivors of the Pima village alliance. The guide, the German, Jack Davidson, John Brewer, and Adams were led away by fate to a continuation of their lives. These five were the originators of the Adams legend. It was their expedition; the experience and the adventure belonged to them. Now, their words and the gold are all that remain.

It may well be that descendants of those five survivors are living today. If so, they could possess information that, if used with modern understanding, just might help to unravel this enduring mystery and point the way to the gold. Such a procedure, though, will not come from dust-gathering documents any quicker than it will from disinterested descendants.

The Pima-Mexican Guide

Among the more appealing aspects of the legend are those segments of the early accounts that describe the people involved and what has been written about them. For instance, the guide for the expedition was not only Indian, but he was of mixed blood. As stated earlier, his mother was a Pima Indian and his father was a Mexican. As their offspring, he had no particular claim to either culture.

Adding to his unusual status was his abduction, at a young age, by the Apaches, yet a third cultural influence on his life. By his story, we know that he came to hate his abductors and eventually broke away from them. With that background, it is not likely that he would have been greatly influenced by their tribal laws or customs. In this respect, he was definitely the exception, not the rule, as most of his Apache brothers were subject to such laws and customs. In many ways, this almost total lack of cultural ties proved to be no detriment to him. In fact, the adversities he suffered as a child appear to have strengthened him.

Of all the men the miners could have come into contact with, this young half-breed not only knew about the rich gold deposits, but was probably one of the few people living who possessed that knowledge and was not afraid to discuss the subject with white men. In addition, he was also fully capable of meeting the responsibilities involved in guiding the miners to the gold. When one further considers the fact that these unique characteristics belonged to a young man no more than half the age of the miners, it becomes quite clear how unusual he was.

How this independent Pima-Mexican youth could have convinced twenty-two miners to make such an effort will remain a mystery; but this also takes him out of the ordinary and into the rare.

Guide them he did. And by that guidance, the miners entered into an adventure that has now become one of the classic gold mining legends of all time. It is interesting that the tragic end to the endeavor took place only after the Pima-Mexican's guidance ceased. When he left the gold camp that night and rode into the darkness, it was the end of him as far as the record of this expedition is concerned.

There were rumors that he was killed by the Apaches not long after he left the miners' camp. Indians were reportedly seen riding the horses that were given to him, but this has never been verified.

For his years, he was far above average in intelligence. He was healthy, resourceful, and knew the Apaches. If the Indians did kill him, it was probably by means of yet another ambush. Of course, it is just as possible that the young Pima-Mexican was not killed at all. In considering this possibility, we tend to think that he would simply have returned home to the Pima villages.

Legend tells us, however, that he was alone, his parents having been killed many years before. He had traveled far and wide with his Apache abductors. It would not be the first time that such traveling, at so young an age, had instilled wanderlust in a developing young man.

At that point, he was far better off than he had ever been in his life. Because of his contract with the miners, he had gold in his pockets, a good horse, and most of his life ahead of him. He could have gone anywhere. This of course, is pure conjecture on my part, but consider the opportunity presented to this young man as a result of his arrangement with the miners. He possessed then the very things that could have given him the world on a silver platter. He had youth, intelligence, a map in his head to a place where gold was incredibly abundant, and he had a pack animal to carry it out for him. It would be fascinating, indeed, to know the rest of his story.

In any event, it is quite possible that he did go to a more attractive locale. If so, it would explain something to me that I have wondered about for a long time. When Adams returned many years later in an attempt to find his old strike again, on at least one occasion his effort began at the Pima villages where the adventure had originally begun.

If his former guide had returned to Sacaton from that first venture, why did Adams not contact him to act as guide again? Naturally, there could be several explanations for this, not the least of which was the youth's death at the hands of the Indians who killed most of the miners.

My purpose for introducing this line of thought is simply to point out that no proof of the guide's untimely demise exists. It is possible that he lived a long life, raised a family, and left descendants unto this day.

The German

Many tales exist about the fate of the German. About all we really know with any degree of certainty, however, is that he apparently did go out with the men in the supply party. After leaving them, he was to take the back trail to Arizona alone. He had become increasingly fearful of the Indians, fear that was not shared by the other miners. To this Dutchman, staying indefinitely in the canyon was a life-threatening situation. Riding the back trail alone was dangerous, but to him it was the lesser of two evils. It is doubtful that he ever knew how right he was.

Without any doubt, the best articulation of the legend was written by J. Frank Dobie in his fine book, *Apache Gold and Yaqui Silver.* Much of Dobie's research involved a generation of people, some of whom were living when the search for the Lost Adams began. From that generation, by way of Dobie's words, we learn that there is more than one version of the German's fate.

One of these versions involved a man by the name of Bob Lewis. Lewis was a resident of Socorro and Magdalena, New Mexico. For many years he was a part-time searcher for the Adams gold. With specific regard to the German, I respectfully quote from page 59 of *Apache Gold and Yaqui Silver.*

> On one of his many prospecting trips into the Datil Mountains, Lewis fell in with an old Navajo chief named Secretare—a kind of renegade to his tribe. Riding along, they came upon the disintegrated skeleton of a man. It had evidently been weathering for many years. "That is

the damned German," old Secretare grunted—and said nothing else. He seemed to know.[1]

Dobie went on to relate the Charles Allen Account (as is reviewed in our Chapter 1), stating that the German went back to Arizona and sold his gold. Then he started a cattle ranch with a brother near Prescott. That report claims the Dutchman was killed on his ranch by Apaches in 1867. Yet another account told of his return to Germany where he lived out the remainder of his life in comfort from the proceeds of his gold. Little more is known of this man, and now time has closed the door.

Jack Davidson

The third man on this list of survivors is the elderly gentleman known as Davidson. In the Allen Account, he is called Jack Davidson.

After their successful escape, Adams and Davidson eventually got back into the White Mountains and onto the trail that they had followed from Sacaton. According to the Allen Account, keeping near their old route, they made it back to a location near the place where Fort Apache was later located. There, the two were picked up by a troop of cavalry scouts out of Fort Whipple, Arizona. This is where Adams and Davidson parted company.

Once more, Adams was besieged by Indian problems. Davidson went on to Fort Whipple with the scouts where he remained for a time. At the fort, he told essentially the same story that was later given out by Adams about the expedition, the canyon, and the gold.

Apparently, Davidson was not the salesman that Adams proved to be, as there does not appear to be any record of his having convinced others to back him in an attempt to return for the gold. In fact, quite the opposite might have been the case.

A man named Kirkpatrick would have supplied just such backing had it not been for ridicule suffered at the hands of skeptics. They called Davidson *Crazy Jack* and laughingly talked Kirkpatrick out of his support.[2] In giving in to that teasing, Kirkpatrick might have made the biggest mistake of his life. This was just one more in a series of developments that seemed destined to block any further exploitation of the canyon of gold.

During his stay at Fort Whipple, Davidson told his story to many, but few believed him, and those who did were of no consequence. Whatever the level of disbelief his listeners may have held, Davidson did tell his version, and that story became part of the Allen Account.

John Brewer

John Brewer was the fourth survivor of the alliance. His story is not only interesting, but it is also the best collaboration of Adams' incredible tale. Most of the information about this man and his version of the Adams gold strike comes from A.M. Tenney, Jr.[3]

Over twenty years had come and gone since Brewer first ventured into the Little Colorado River country near the area that came to be known as Round Valley and later Springerville, Arizona. He returned in the late 1880s, this time with quite a different outfit.

Instead of the long column of riders as on the first occasion, he had an Indian wife, a daughter, two covered wagons, and a few head of livestock. Living off the land as he came, he had made his way down from Colorado. In recent years, he had tried farming and had not done badly at it. However, he could never forget what he had once seen.

He was possessed by thoughts of gold, and longed to see that special canyon, with its unusual fireplace vault.

Brewer had been away from the New Mexico frontier for a long time. To some degree, he had been in seclusion, pursuing life as a farmer. He had, therefore, never heard the stories spread far and wide by Adams. Indeed, Brewer was not even aware that Adams or anyone else had escaped the massacres. He believed that he alone survived. His story, as preserved for us by Tenney, tells about the events of that fateful day, starting with that terrifying, surprise attack by the raiders.

It all began with what seemed to Brewer like an unusual sound. For just a brief moment, he failed to identify the thud of many horses' hooves as they pounded down the sandy floor of the canyon, a sound not unlike that of stampeding cattle. Perhaps it was the simple improbability of hearing such a sound that confused him.

As quickly as possible, he found an elevated place from which he could survey the area. It took only a few seconds for Brewer to realize that the camp was under attack by a large number of Indians. Acting instinctively, he dropped out of sight behind a ridge; then, mostly by crawling, managed to work his way away from the death site.

He heard the air-splitting screams as his companions died at the hands of their executioners. Frantically, he looked for cover, a place to hide from the sudden threat. Then he found it, a cedar tree with thick boughs pushed up against a bank, and into the cover he went. He lay there, hour after hour, expecting any second to be discovered since riders, on more than one occasion, came dangerously close. Brewer lay wrapped in the arms of that cedar tree until day finally faded into night.

In his mind, he reasoned that the raiding Indians had hit the provisions party as well. Then he remembered Adams and the old fellow Davidson and how they had left camp, even before sunup, to look for the boys in the incoming supply party.

Brewer's thoughts were a reflection of his mood: *They're all dead, everyone has been butchered—everyone but me and soon I'll be dead too!*

With the darkness came a little security. As Brewer lay there, it became obvious, from the muffled sound of the Indians chanting their victory song, that he had managed to put a little distance between himself and them. He turned on his side and looked in the direction of the chanting. Through the bleak darkness, he could see a reddish glow above the trees and rocks.

Well, there goes the cabin, he thought to himself.

Then it occurred to him that the victory rites would keep the Indians busy for a while and that gave him a slim thread of hope. Slipping out of his cover, he inched away from the area. Once he paused to check for his sidearm but found only an empty holster. In crawling away from camp that morning, the gun had apparently fallen out.

Like a cold chill, it came over him how desperate his situation had become. The only trail leading back to civilization was the trail that led to Fort Wingate, and Brewer suspected the Indians would be watching it closely.

Even by horseback, it was four days' travel back to the fort, and he had no horse. There was no other civilization, as he knew it, nothing but the settlements along the Rio Grande.

That could be a hundred miles! He just did not know. Once more, panic threatened. He was afoot with no gun, no water or food, not even matches. *Might as well be dead!* The life saving darkness of night that only a short while ago had sheltered him now filled his soul with bewildering despair.

Then, from out of nowhere, came a sign of hope. The biggest moon he had ever seen was just breaking over a distant mesa. Suddenly he knew where east was; somewhere out there, toward that moon, was the Rio Grande.

By degrees, despair gave way to resolution. Brewer could almost hear his own thoughts: *I will not die here! I have been spared! I will survive!*

All at once, life was more precious than he had ever imagined. Somehow he would make it. It was a long shot. The odds were set against him from the beginning, but the sight of that moon was like a hand reaching out of the night to help him. He turned his back on the reddish glow of the death camp and started walking toward the moon—and toward the rest of his life.

Brewer had no idea how far it was to the river, but one thing was for sure—that river meant settlements of people. That thought gave him purpose and reason; in these, he found the strength to go on. He traveled then, sometimes in the daylight, but mostly at night, ever fearful of the Indians.

His route took him over one of the most barren and desolate districts in the Southwest. Springs were scattered far apart in the mountainous areas, but they disappeared completely many miles west of the Rio Grande where the terrain was predominantly desert. Somewhere in that arid portion Brewer's strength finally gave out.

He had made it to a well-traveled trail, which he followed to an arroyo. Water flowed along the floor of the gully, and he dropped to his knees to get a drink of water, then collapsed. He might well have died there had it not been for three Indian males who found him and took him to their nearby home.

His story tells us about an Indian family that fed him and nourished him back to good health. From them, Brewer learned that he was not far from a pueblo headed by an Indian *gobernador* (governor) and an alcalde. The alcalde was a magistrate who was sent out from the territorial capital in Santa Fe.

Alcaldes were active at all the pueblos of that period. Their purpose was that of a judge in settling disputes between members of a village. They worked with the pueblo governor and tribal council, but they were also a representative of the territorial governor in Sante Fe.

When Brewer had recuperated enough, he went to the pueblo to confer with the tribal council and the alcalde. There, he hoped to enlist the help of the residents in forming a party to return to the massacre site. He wanted to go back to check for any indication of other survivors and to bury the dead. Because of the death of so many, his own miraculous escape and the experience in general, the value Brewer had once placed on gold had diminished greatly. He would not return for the gold alone.

After hearing him out, the Indians would have no part of such a plan. They had experienced a great deal of trouble with the Apaches, and as a result refused to consider Brewer's proposal. They were understanding but firm on this point.

The Indians did tell him about a military post that was some distance to the west. They suggested that the soldiers might provide assistance. Here again, the country toward the fort was a dangerous area frequented by roving bands of Apache and Navajo, and the Pueblo Indians would not enter it. Brewer reasoned that they meant Fort Wingate, but there was no way he would attempt to reach the fort alone.

According to Brewer, the Pueblo Indians treated him well. They offered to take him to other Indian villages, or guide him to the Rio Grande. Just across the river, on the east side, were the settlements he had started out to reach. There he would also find the Chihuahua Trail and freighters bound for Sante Fe. When he had sufficiently recovered, he resumed his journey to the Rio Grande and civilization.

Although he had little in his pockets, he still had those gold coins he had once shown to the half-breed guide. With these, he purchased clothes and shoes in one of the river villages.

Brewer spent three days in the village before getting work with an outfit traveling to Santa Fe. After a few days in the capital, he signed on with a wagon train on its way back to Missouri. Eventually, he did return to the west, to Colorado, where he started farming.

This is essentially the story he told A.M. Tenney, Jr.

For several months, Brewer, Tenney, and some of the local ranchers searched for landmarks that would mean something to Brewer, but they found nothing. Headquarters for the search was the Tenney farm, on the Little Colorado River, just a few miles north of present day Springerville, Arizona.

Three or four years earlier, another man came to the Tenney farm looking for the same old trail. This was Captain C. A. Shaw, another seeker of the Adams gold, whose undying interest in the lost mine had been generated by Adams himself. Captain Shaw had already made many searches, starting with Adams. His intention now was the same as Brewer's—to find that old original trail.

Both of these adventurers found this task beyond their abilities, however, and, consequently, neither was able to locate the old route. Too many years had gone by, something stood in the way, and the mystery lived on.

The fact that both Brewer and Shaw came to this location, near Springerville, is of some importance in its own right. Obviously, Brewer thought it was near the old route. Shaw, going on what he had learned from Adams himself, had arrived at the same conclusion.

Brewer, the fourth survivor, represents the fourth channel for possible descendants.

Adams

Without a doubt, Adams became the most celebrated of the five survivors. His life after the massacres became a testament to the incredible adventure of which he had been so much a part.

When he and Davidson made contact with the cavalry scouts in eastern Arizona, both men were in bad shape from prolonged exposure. The two were physically and mentally exhausted. After being examined by one in the troop who had medical training, they were given food and supplied with a tent.

Then, the weary pair turned in for much needed rest. However, it turned out to be a troubled sleep. Adams was so tired that he tossed and turned, unable to adjust to the comfort and security. Suddenly, he heard noises outside the tent.

In a half-conscious state, he grabbed his gun, threw open a flap on the front of the tent, and looked out to see mounted Indians. He fired, quickly emptying his gun, and two of the red men fell dead. The Indians were not troublemakers; they were there simply to talk to the scouts.

Once more, Adams found himself in dire straits. An officer in charge of the scout party placed Adams under arrest and told him he would be taken back to Fort Whipple for trial. Before the party reached the fort, however, Adams escaped on one of the unit's horses. In the weeks that followed, he made his way to his home in California.

At that time, Adams had all he wanted of Apacheria. First, his very existence was nothing short of a miracle. His escape from the canyon was a fluke, a one-in-a-million chance. He had to face that untamed country while stripped of the essentials for life, to the point of starvation. He had become demoralized by the events that simply overwhelmed both himself and his partner Davidson.

Then, after being rescued by white men, and once more witnessing the emotion of hope, he saw that hope crushed by his own violence in the killing of the two peaceful Indians. Suddenly, in an entirely new situation, he found himself a fugitive from justice.

Adams had been exposed to a phenomenal series of peaks and valleys in his life; the exposure had come by an almost rhythmic chain of events. The most important by-product of his experience was the creation of a strong, durable, and impressive individual, who was capable of convincing many other men of the truth of his story. The result of this was the propagation of that story into the legend that it eventually became.

Adams, like Brewer, could never forget what he had once seen. His case of gold fever became unique. It did not help when most of the talk in California would either start or end concerning gold. Because of gold, California had flashed into the limelight of the nation in the great gold rush of 1849.

Still, Adams had lived through such an appalling nightmare that, at first, nothing could entice him back. There are accounts of his coming down with typhoid fever and nearly dying. This would have left him disheartened, and thereby prolonged any plans he may have held for making a return. Eventually, the all-consuming lust took possession of him, and he tried to get the necessary backing for his own attempt at reclaiming the old strike.

To say the acquisition of such backing was an uphill battle would be stating it mildly. California, then in a state of rapid development, still had more than its share of gold mining and the industries that were associated with it. Here was a poor man trying to promote a gold mining operation in New Mexico. That gold mine was something he had seen once, something he would have to relocate, and it was also in what some people called hostile Indian country, a long way from the California strikes.

We can only surmise that he must have been a master at persuasion. More than once, this talent resulted in the organization of large expeditions. It is thought by many that the first of these trips occurred in the mid-1870s. Adams led another long column of riders out of southern California, across the deserts of southern Arizona Territory, to the Pima villages. There, he hoped to follow the route that his former guide had taken.

Some three to four weeks later, this accumulation of hopefuls had made it to the newly founded settlement of Milligan Plaza on the San Francisco River in southwestern New Mexico. Needless to say, they did not find the canyon of gold.

However, Adams did see something in this area that he thought he had seen on his first trip. Whatever he saw brought him back into the San Francisco River country many times. On one of those trips, he found his way to Cox Canyon, not far from Reserve (the former Milligan Plaza), and to Mrs. Ben E. Kemp's father's cabin where he told her father about the gold strike.[4]

On another occasion, Adams and his backers worked their way out of California, across the Colorado River, and into the northeastern part of Arizona, a far cry from the San Francisco River. He spent several months in northern Arizona, but found nothing of his old trail to the gold.

Looking at these two search areas now, it is difficult to understand how a man could become so confused, given that the two regions are extremely far apart. In defense of Adams, however, one might point out that both regions have many similarities. Both have mountainous areas in which the general topography of the country is quite comparable.

Something else occurred to me when I tried to understand his effort in northern Arizona. It could be that, knowing the original trail bore northeast through the White Mountains, Adams was just overshooting the destination he had in mind. Quite possibly, his intention was to intercept the old trail north of Escudilla Mountain. If that was the case, he missed it by a surprising distance.

Here again, when trying to judge what happened, we must always keep in mind how much this country has changed. There was no Interstate 40 then; no Winslow, Holbrook, or Gallup. The Navajos were there, along with the Hopi and Zuni Tribes, but they were fewer in number. As for the Anglos, Fort Defiance was the only white outpost in all of northeastern Arizona. There was not even a fence post to break the natural environment.

Adams did not have a road map; he crossed Arizona without ever seeing a center stripe. When he looked up from his horse to survey the country in front of him, all he saw was mile after mile of deserts and mountains, valleys and forests. It was fascinating and beautiful, but also extremely repetitious.

Adams is reported to have been seen in Silver City, Lake Valley, Alma, Magdalena, and Fort Wingate in New Mexico. He also covered portions of eastern Arizona using Fort Apache as his supply point. He tried desperately to reclaim his lost canyon strike. In pursuit of that quest, he talked to people all across the Southwest, trying to find someone who had seen one of those landmarks he remembered so clearly.

It is not hard to imagine his locating someone, every once in a while, who knew right where the two haystack peaks were, or the long bluff. How disappointed he must have been, at such times, when it did not pan out.

All of the texts agree that Adams was easily disoriented. He was the type of person who quickly lost his sense of direction when exposed to a new or unfamiliar environment. This flaw was probably responsible for part of his inability to recognize, at some point, the old trail he sought. Through the years when he returned and searched, there were probably times that he did cross that trail and simply did not recognize it.

Another thing that may have been detrimental to his effort was the taking of an occasional drink, although it is hard to believe that Adams was an overindulgent drunk. For one thing, he impressed many people most favorably. Some of them trusted and respected him for years.

By all accounts, Adams was far from wealthy. Perhaps a wealthy man could get away with excessive drinking and still impress others; money talks, but such is not the case with a poor man. Adams was a poor man with a golden dream that needed monetary backing. No, he was not a drunk. An occasional drinker is the way he was described by many who knew him, but it is difficult to say what effect, if any, this may have had on efforts to relocate the canyon of gold.

How many times Adams might have been in contact with the old trail will never be known, nor will his state of alertness at such times be revealed. If Adams was addicted to anything, it was the quest. His first love was the hope of finding the burned-out cabin where he could slide aside the heavy hearthstone that he had once helped to set in place.

Adams was many things: an adventurer, a killer when he had to be, and he was influential. He may have been greedy, but he was also generous in promising a portion of the gold to those who were willing to share his effort. It was once said of Adams that he would have given up long before he did had it not been for those shares he promised to the many who had faith in him. In truth, he never gave up until a heart problem arose while he was still on the search.

Adams can be described as a durable and persistent man; a rugged individualist. Yet at the same time, we recognize that our John Wayne-type is something of a paradox in that he was cursed by a poor sense of direction.

In *Apache Gold and Yaqui Silver*, Dobie states that Adams came to his death in 1886.[5] He was stricken by a heart attack while in New Mexico on another searching trip. He was taken to the southern part of the state and put on a train for California. There, in his Los Angeles home, he passed away in September of that year. His death came only after much effort, many searches that involved a great array of people, and a great deal of agonizing disappointment.

It has been said that timing is everything, and that expression was never truer than in this man's life. Following the burning of his freight wagons, four events, because of their unusual timing, produced the legend. The events were the direct result of decisions Adams made. The decisions were his, but they were made out of necessity in response to situations and circumstances over which Adams had little or no control.

The first of these four events took place when Adams entered into the Pima village alliance. It was his decision to take the wagon teams into the village in search of a buyer. It was also his decision to try for the half-breed's gold. Looking back from this perspective, it hardly seems that Adams had much choice.

The second event occurred when Adams and Davidson escaped being killed in the massacres that took place at the canyon of gold. A decision by Adams provided that early morning deliverance, the decision to go out and look for that ill-fated provisions party. They were, after all, overdue.

Then came the killing of the two Indians in the camp of the scouts in Arizona. That was yet another decision, albeit, made by a man half asleep. Still, who would not have done the same thing if the conditions and circumstances were as Adams had them? His reaction, while not justifiable, was certainly understandable.

Important is the fact that had this incident not occurred, it is likely that Adams and Davidson would have been able to persuade the post commander at Fort Whipple to give them an escort back to the canyon. With the country still fresh in their minds, the two of them could probably have retraced their steps. If this had happened there would be no legend. In making Adams a fugitive from justice, this third event surely contributed to his delayed return to search for the gold and thereby became responsible for his ultimate failure.

The last event, which certainly proved to be important to Adams and his story, was his meeting a man who would continue the quest long after Adams had died. Captain Shaw, while not a survivor of the original adventure, definitely takes a seat next to Adams when it comes to establishing credibility for this long-enduring tradition.

Such is the story of what is known of the survivors. As a result of their efforts in this great adventure, these five witnessed an astonishing occurrence of one of the world's rarest metallic elements.

That element has been coveted and cherished by man from the dawn of his enlightened civilizations. Most of that element (that has been found) remains in guarded vaults throughout the world. Down through time, thousands have died in the effort to own or control it. Each of these stories has its own survivors.

3

THE FACTS—A CLOSER LOOK

The history of the United States is filled with both positive and negative periods. One of her darkest hours was the decade of the 1860s when the country was shaken by the ravages of the Civil War. Southern states were brought to their knees by defeat and by the devastating aftermath that followed. Thousands died; for millions, their way of life was changed forever.

Internal pressures created by the great conflict needed a vent. That escape was found, in part, in the developing western frontier. Just the name *California* became a new hope for the future, while thoughts of gold fanned the flames of that hope and triggered a vast movement west. One after another, the stars of Old Glory were beginning to shine.

Thus was the climate of the day. Easterners, with all their frailties and strengths, were suddenly thrust against those of western cultures—and the frontier heated up. While war was not a forgotten thing of the East; the West also became a place of violence. Part of the price of greatness that did become America was paid, year in and year out, in the exploding collision of the cultures. This was the time frame and the atmosphere. For our story, the moment was right.

I wondered, as I suspect everyone who hears about or reads about the Adams story wonders, could this really have happened? In an effort to establish credibility, I took a closer look at the facts that have been written down by so many, for so long.

The Pima Village

According to most of the early writers, the story originated in the Pima Indian villages of south central Arizona Territory. Precisely which Pima village is not clear. The accounts simply say the Pima village or villages. In our narrative, we are taking Sacaton as that village because of its centralized location and its history of being a point of supply for travelers on their way to and from California.

In a real sense, it was an oasis in the desert. Dating back for many centuries, the Pima people have been a part of the historical record of the Southwest, much longer than the Spanish or the Americans.

From the time of the first Spanish conquistadors, over four hundred years ago, the Pimas have maintained a friendly and peaceful relationship with the Hispanic and Caucasian people with whom they have come in contact.

In all probability, the outfitting of a party of twenty-three men for such an undertaking as the Adams expedition would have drawn on the resources of several of the closely situated Pima villages. If that was the case, Sacaton would have been the logical staging point. It was also the place where Adams would have taken his wagon teams.

The Mining Party

Would twenty-one miners have traveled together across the desert southwest in 1864? Here, one need only acquire some basic knowledge of American history.

The country was split by revolution. The Civil War was in its fourth year. It was becoming increasingly evident that the Confederacy could not survive much longer. There were over 300,000 deserters from the war; about a third of whom were desperate Southerners who had lost everything as a result of the conflict.

Large bands of men were crossing the country then. In some cases, those groups contained far more than twenty men at a time. Prospecting and mining precious metals throughout the west were enticing incentives, as was homesteading. Thus, in 1864, there was nothing unusual about this particular mining party.

Adams—the Freighter

During the nineteenth century, one of the most important access routes to the new western frontier was the Santa Fe Trail to New Mexico. From Santa Fe, the route went south along the Rio Grande over what had come to be known as *El Camino Real* (Royal Road) or the Chihuahua Trail. On that route, travelers could go to El Paso (and on into Chihuahua, Mexico) or they could take the old Butterfield Trail across the southern portions of New Mexico and Arizona to California.

This route was followed by more travelers because it was more conducive to travel during the winter months. Because of this, stagecoach lines were established, mail routes were developed, and freighters such as Adams began serving that region.

The southwestern New Mexico portion of the old Butterfield Trail was, in many places, the forerunner of today's Interstate Highway 10. Manufactured goods were moved from the eastern states to California by means of horse-drawn wagons, a practice that continued for many years, until supplanted by the railroad. These were the first teamsters, and Adams' story of being one of them is feasible.

The Half-breed Guide

The young half-breed's story was unusual, but far from unprecedented. Many books on Indian tribes tell of the capture of children by renegade groups. That subjugation was the result of raids on villages, farms, and wagon trains, in which the parents were killed and their offspring left homeless. Mexican, Indian, and Anglo children were known to have grown to adulthood in such groups. The Pima-Mexican guide was one of those children. Upon becoming a young man, he escaped his captors.

In every account, this youthful half-breed was described as an exceptional person. He was outgoing and popular with the miners he guided. Although young, he was also equal to his job. Despite his youth, he had apparently learned much about life. Such experience could have been acquired while living as a child of renegade Apache subjugation.

The Alliance

Gold brought these people together and was the bond of their alliance, a not unusual relationship. Indeed, the arrangement between these men was far from unbelievable. All the ingredients were there. The twenty-one miners represented the necessary expertise in mining. Adams, because of the loss of his wagons, had an excess of horses that allowed him to provide the much needed transportation. The young Pima-Mexican? He knew where the gold was. All things considered, it could have happened just that way—and that is one of the reasons why this story became a legend.

The reaction of these men to gold is interesting. Adams, though not a miner, was something of an adventurer; and gold appealed to this side of his nature. The miners were elated at the sight of small nuggets called float gold that they had discovered nearby.

Float gold is a term used to describe the metal in either a nugget or in dust form that has broken free from its matrix rock. To a prospector or miner, float gold is a fascinating find, an indication of what might turn out to be an accumulation. Most gold that has been mined has been acquired by means of hard-rock mining, i.e., the crushing of many tons of ore-bearing materials in order to extract only ounces of the precious metal.

While finding the little nuggets had greatly excited the miners, the young Pima-Mexican was not impressed. Noteworthy here is the fact that the half-breed was on his own ground. The miners were the outsiders, travelers on a trip, just passing through. They did, however, know all about gold: how to look for it, what rock it occurred in, and what it was worth. The youthful half-breed knew none of these things, but he did know gold when he saw it.

Here was a peaceful meeting of the cultures, with a coming together of ideas by those of different backgrounds. The breed had laughed at the miners' elation, thinking they were engaging in some sort of joke. In his mind, he wondered how those tiny fragments could seriously impress anyone. He had seen the metal before and thought the nuggets the miners had to be worthless indeed.

How many times he had seen gold in its native form will never be known, but one of those times was spectacular. At one point, gold had impressed him, so much so that now he could, by the description of what he had seen, convey that impression to others.

In trying to further my own understanding of how this young half-breed could have convinced so many of his tale of gold, a closer look took me once more to Byerts' text. In his article, Byerts asserts that the half-breed who became the guide for the miners had a reputation of being honest and truthful. If he told a person something, it could be relied on, according to the other Indians at the Pima village where he lived.[1] Apparently, his word was trusted by all who knew him. This trait, rare then as now, was obviously recognized by the mining partners.

Still, I felt there was probably more to his case than simply his word. Of course, it is possible that he had some nuggets, which would certainly have helped his credibility. But maybe there was something else. Information the miners could have had would have made it easier to believe the half-breed. As prospectors and miners, they would likely have been aware of current gold mining activity in the Territory, as well as where past gold strikes had taken place.

In 1828, gold was rediscovered at the Old Placers in the Ortiz Mountains northeast of Albuquerque, a site once worked by Spaniards. This discovery became the first important gold strike west of the Mississippi River. In the spring of 1829, the area of the Old Placers was besieged by gold hunters and a major rush developed. This event is considered by many to have opened the eyes of the world to the possibility of great mineral wealth in the Rocky Mountain region. For many years, this strike gave up a phenomenal amount of gold.

Between 1828 and 1864, gold was found in scattered placers around the territories of New Mexico and

Arizona. Those occurrences were probably in the thoughts of the miners when the half-breed told his story. This would have helped them keep an open mind when it came to the subject of gold deposits, accumulations of which were waiting to be discovered in the uncharted reaches of the southwest frontier.

Direction of the Route

In retelling his story, there were many points on which Adams never varied. One of those was the direction of the course taken by the party from the beginning until they reached the canyon of gold. That direction was northeast. It would be interesting to know how many times over the last century maps have been laid out in an attempt to establish the expedition's route and the place they reached.

To go exactly northeast of the Pima village of Sacaton, the line would come extremely close to Snowflake, Arizona. It would then pass near the city of Gallup, New Mexico, and onward, toward what is now Chaco Culture National Historic Park.

I do not believe it is unreasonable to say that when Adams used the term *northeast,* it was intended more as a general reference than as a precise point on the compass. Springerville, Arizona, which most writers agree was near the old trail, is in reality on a line closer to the direction of east-northeast from the Pima village location.

Give that same margin for error to the north side of northeast and what develops is a search area over 150 miles across at its outer perimeter. With this bit of information, we can factor in another reason why this old story about gold reached legendary proportions.

While it is true that none of the accounts offer detailed directions on how to find the gold discovery canyon, some come closer to doing this than others. Of these, the Byerts version, quoting Adams, comes closer than most.

> According to Adams, the course they took from the Pima villages in Arizona would land the Adams "diggings" in the northern part of Socorro county, or a little north of this, as the point of the Malpai mountains is in Socorro county.[2]

Socorro County was in existence in 1864 although its boundary lines were little more than guesswork. It extended from east to west, completely spanning the Territory of New Mexico. In the years since, the county boundaries have changed considerably with the exception of that original northern line. It is the same today as it was in 1864.

Catron County, of which Reserve (Milligan Plaza) is the county seat, was created out of Socorro County on its western side. The northern boundary of these two counties was once the northern county line of the original Socorro County, or that part of it extending from the Rio Grande to the Arizona border.

In saying the "diggin's" should be in the northern part of Socorro County, Adams was talking about another area much closer to the direction of east-northeast of the Pima villages than it is true-northeast. That area, the country along the northern Socorro County-Catron County lines, is a long way from northeastern Arizona; and it is also a considerable distance from the San Francisco River and Reserve, New Mexico. Once more, this points out the wide-ranging search conducted by Adams and those who were with him.

The Point of the Malpais

Another part of the Byerts' quotation is vital. In addition to discussing the Socorro County line, Adams also brings up the *Point of the Malpais*. This is a landmark that has been well known in western New Mexico since the days of the Spanish occupation. Physically, it is the fingerlike, southernmost extension of a massive lava flow. That flow reaches over thirty-five miles to the south from the Old Fort Wingate location near Grants. It has now been established as the El Malpais National Monument and El Malpais National Conversation Area.

Within the monument are ice caves that have floors of never-melting ice; there are many volcanic craters (inactive for thousands of years) that originally spewed forth the molten rock. Since that time, Native Americans have developed trails across the endless miles of dangerously sharp, blackened layers of stone. Travel across the Malpais, beyond those trails, becomes extremely difficult. The Spanish explorers first called the area El Malpais (the badlands), and it is so called to this day.

The first time the *Point of the Malpais* is brought up in the Byerts text, Adams was recalling the words of the guide. He was instructing the miners about the route they would have to take to get to the fort for supplies. He told them to follow the *wagon road,* they had just crossed, *east* to the *Point of the Malpais.* They would then travel northward to Fort Wingate.[3]

This set of directions in the Byerts article needed only to have been wrong by one word to have completely changed public opinion regarding the most logical place to look for the lost canyon.

Consider the fact that Adams was looking back many years to when he first heard the guide's words. Adams, whose sense of direction was notably poor, said

State Highway 117, Along the "Point of the Malpais."

(according to Byerts), "east . . . to the *Point of the Malpais.*"

Further instructions in this article left no doubt that the location of the rich strike was in the Malpais Mountains. In 1916, when the Byerts article first appeared, those instructions were exciting and full of promise; because of this, many searchers entered that section with great expectations. Now, however, with over seventy years of hindsight, that excitement is gone; the better odds are that the instructions were wrong to begin with—possibly wrong at the outset—by the word *east.*

Be that as it may, perhaps the most important thing about these words in the Byerts text is the fact the young guide had spoken of this noted landmark. If this part of Adams' revelation was true, and the guide did speak about the *Point of the Malpais,* then that landmark becomes important, indeed.

One other puzzling thing concerning these thoughts about the noted malpais landmark is the total absence of any discussion about Mt. Taylor, another prominent landmark approximately fifty miles north-northeast of the malpais point. Rising to a summit exceeding eleven thousand feet, it was known as Mt. Taylor even in 1864. With its elevation in the region unchallenged, it was then, and it is now, the most obvious landmark in western New Mexico.

It would seem that Adams should have used Mt. Taylor to get his bearings when he came back on his own searches, but there is no evidence he did. Could it be that while following the young guide, the mining party never saw Mt. Taylor? If they, indeed, did not, that fact becomes significant. It could mean their incoming route did not lend itself to views of the mountain. That in turn, would eliminate some sections of New Mexico which were once the settings of many searches for the lost canyon. If the provisions party went into Old Fort Wingate, they would have seen Mt. Taylor. However, they were all killed.

Indian Trails and Routes

Another point on which Adams was consistent was the fact that the party was moving on well established Indian trails. To any visitor of the beautiful White Mountains of Arizona, it is hard to imagine crossing the region on horseback and getting very far in a single day. The terrain appears to be so interlaced with ridges and canyons that such travel would seem to be extremely time consuming.

The Apaches and other Native American inhabitants of the region had centuries to develop many trails making it possible to move with some degree of expediency. The world of the Apaches posed few deadlines or time limits. Theirs was, of course, a much slower paced life style than that of today. Still, there were times when they were motivated to cross stretches of land faster than they would normally travel.

Apacheria was an immense region; crossing it, from one portion to another, could best be accomplished on established trails. In many cases, those trails simply led from one watering place to another. Trails also covered long distances and connected the outlying districts of Apacheria with the White Mountain homeland.

The mining expedition used these existing Indian trails in its passage through the White Mountains.

Mt. Ord to Springerville Location

Old accounts tell about that first expedition from the Mt. Ord area to the location of present day Springerville taking only two days. This would be difficult to accomplish even on a direct route; in the Allen Account, Adams told of following what he thought was Nutrioso Creek out of the mountains.[4] If that is true, such a trip would require an eastward movement from their camp above the East Fork to Nutrioso Creek and then northward to the lower elevation area now known as the town of Springerville.

On the face of it, it looks like a ride of several days to Springerville going that way. For a time, I was puzzled by this. Then, on a close examination of topographical maps of the area I was surprised to find a logical passage following the same route Adams had described.

A ridge drops off to the east from Mt. Baldy and descends moderately in an eastward disposition to within two miles or so of Crescent Lake. At that point, the ridge terminates into comparatively level terrain. By staying with this level terrain for about twelve miles, access to Nutrioso Creek can be gained. That access comes by dropping into and following the canyon of Auger Creek to its confluence with Nutrioso Creek. The juncture of these two streams occurs near the little village of Nutrioso, from where the valley of Nutrioso Creek drops gradually to the north toward Springerville.

If Adams could ride his old trail today, he would be surprised to find that highway engineers have followed this Nutrioso Creek portion when they determined the route of U.S. Highway 180. The highway leaves the creek about five miles from Springerville and makes a north-westward turn toward that city. Nutrioso Creek then continues northward and crosses U.S. Highway 60 *two miles* east of Springerville, a location that was previously mentioned as being one of the Adams party's campsites. This route is downhill in its entirety, and it is quite possible that the trip could be accomplished in two days. It would result in a campsite near and to the east of Springerville.

A Dry Camp

If one travels east, northeast, or north from Springerville, he will ultimately cross lava beds, juniper-covered hills, or both. In any case, to cross such terrain without the benefit of a trail takes much longer and water quickly becomes a priority. That need for water is a sure motivation for expediency.

The Adams party had to face this arid desert region. Early writers said that after leaving their Springerville area campsite the miners made at least one dry camp, possibly more. It is quite probable that their first night out into that harsh terrain was spent at one of these dry camps. By those old accounts, from a dry, waterless camp they rode on the following day and reached a running stream of water in the evening. That water flowed to the northwest.

Here again, great distances are involved. To go from the Springerville area to a place with running water by heading east, northeast, or north would require a long ride, and only by riding long hours, over developed trails, could a large party cover such distances quickly. For instance, it is fifty miles over modern U.S. Highway 60 from Springerville to Largo Creek at Quemado; that is the nearest running water, that way.

Most of the streambeds in this desert region are no more than dry arroyos. They run water briefly after showers during the rainy season. Downstream from Quemado, Largo Creek is no exception. It begins, however, several miles south of Quemado in the Mangus Mountains near the continental divide. From there water flows most of the year to a point not far above the village. The water then sinks into sand, and Largo Creek, like most other streams flowing out of the mountains and into the deserts, becomes a dry wash. Even the cottonwood trees stop when the water stops.

Of Negatives and Positives

Something else that could be important at this point involves a negative rather than a positive—another major and unusual landmark about fifty miles northeast of Springerville that Adams should have talked about but did not.

The Zuni Indian Tribe has mined salt in what is reported to be a vast, deep meteoric crater. That mining operation has gone on for hundreds of years. The bottom of the old crater is a lake of salt and water. It is not hard to understand the mining party's missing that crater, a mere dot on the map, but it is quite a different matter to have missed a trail used for literally centuries by the Zunis.

That trail or cart road (because the salt was transported on carts) stretched some fifty miles, north to south, between the Zuni Pueblo and the crater. Due to centuries of use, the cart road would have been as obvious as a rope across the path of anyone traveling northeast or north-northeast from Springerville. I believe that if Adams had seen this cart road he would have told others about it, especially in those later years when the search had claimed most of his life.

However, apart from this line of thought, it seems unlikely that the Zuni cart road would have been the same wagon road that was crossed by the miners, the one their guide had said would lead them to the fort for supplies. For one thing, if the cart road and the wagon road were one and the same, after crossing it, a day's ride on to the northeast would have placed the party that much closer to a major trail that then existed between the Zuni Pueblo and Fort Wingate.

Adams always claimed that their guide instructed the miners to come back to the wagon road and follow it to the fort. He never mentioned the Zunis or their salt trail, an omission he would not reasonably have made.

The Early Roads

The most important trail (or road) in western New Mexico in 1864 was the one referred to above as the major trail between the Zuni Pueblo and Old Fort Wingate—again, this was when Fort Wingate was situated near Grants. Most of that trail, the exception being the portion that came into being as a result of the establishment of Fort Wingate, is now called the Ancient Way that was traveled by Pueblo Indians and Spanish colonials for hundreds of years.

The Ancient Way took a course westward from the Rio Grande, near Albuquerque, to the Acoma Pueblo and across the Malpais south of Fort Wingate. The old highway of the past then proceeded west to El Morro and finally to the Zuni Pueblo. Zuni traders also went farther west on this long trail, deep into what is now Arizona.

In the past, many searchers for the Lost Adams though this well-beaten path might have been the wagon road that the young guide had once pointed out to the miners. As a result, the Zuni Mountain Range that lies to the north of this route has been combed very thoroughly, not only by men on foot but in aircraft as well. Up to now, the whereabouts of the canyon of gold remains a mystery.

Another old trail used by the Navajos for generations and then by everyone, turned northwest from the Fort Wingate area and supplied a route into the Navajo homeland near Fort Defiance and Fort Canby in northeastern Arizona. Much of this trail eventually became the route of New Mexico's Interstate 40 between Grants and Gallup.

Only a few other trails were in use in 1864; the Zuni salt trail and three other Indian routes. These three are part of the story of the last three chapters of this book.

It might be wise to point out here that Adams did not go out with the provisions party. It is also true that he never talked to any of the men who did. The contacts made by the riders in that party as well as the landmarks they saw were never known to Adams. The story he told throughout the West was limited to his own personal experiences.

Somewhere in this general area, the mining party did cross a trail that bore wagon tracks. Obviously, identifying that trail has proven to be an impossible task for

Sign on Highway 53, Southwest of Grants, New Mexico, Designating the "Ancient Way."

those who have attempted to locate it. Apparently, this *wagon road* was the first trail—or at least the first trail of any significance—that the party had come into contact with since leaving the Springerville area camp. From that camp, they had traveled at least two days and part of a third. All of this traveling, according to the Allen Account, was done on well established trails.

Adams said that the course followed by the party was from the southwest to the northeast. If that is true, the trail with the wagon tracks would have to have followed a north-south line to some extent. It is also logical that the crossing of those two trails would have been a fairly important intersection at that time.

The Pumpkin Patch

By most accounts of the story, the group came to what has become known as the Pumpkin Patch within hours after crossing the trail with the wagon tracks. That was another spot, another place in his memory, that Adams never failed to include in his tale of gold.

They had followed the well-traveled trail into a wide basin, through which they had ridden for several hours when suddenly the guide turned away from the main trail and began following a fainter path. Two things happened at this time: Their course was more to the north and the new trail took them out of the wide basin and up onto a tableland.

Adams said they arrived in the evening at a place on the mesa that looked as though it once had been irrigated. Several old, sunken ditches and some vines, possibly pumpkin vines, were seen. In some instances, when he talked about the irrigated patch, he spoke of what looked like dwellings close by. Once more, the men became concerned about Indians, but if there were any in that area, the miners never saw them.

The Long Bluff

Winding in and out of the many variations of the legend can be found the *long bluff* through which the riders eventually passed. The party reached the bluff, or high wall, early in the morning after spending the night in the Pumpkin Patch. According to Adams, the bluff was reddish in color, about sixty to seventy feet high and was quite lengthy.

Throughout western New Mexico, there is a wide range of walls and escarpments. In the mountainous areas of Catron County and the Gila National Forest, there are many walls formed from basaltic outcroppings.

An andesite found extensively in that region also produces high vertical cliffs; many canyons are capped with
it.

Like numerous other formations, the andesite
erodes and weathers and in so doing, exposes iron-con-
taining minerals. This mineral decomposition results in
a rusty coloration that makes an escarpment appear red
from a distance. The capping andesite found in many
canyons makes a descent into them difficult. If one per-
severes, however, he will find a break in the cap, usually within two to three hundred yards and then access is
relatively easy.

In parts of Cibola and McKinley counties, near
Grants and Gallup, there are walls of radically different
materials. In the particular terrain around Gallup and
Zuni, red sandstone formations are prevalent. Bluffs
and canyons are common in the castellated red stone.

The area to the south and southwest of Grants has
seen a great deal of volcanic activity. In the massive lava
flows, there are hills, canyons, and walls that were created in the cooling of the molten rock. Southeast of
Grants, light-colored sandstones form vertical cliffs,
hundreds of feet high in many places. Around the imme-
diate area of Grants, the mesas are capped with walls of
basalt.

By itself, the long red bluff Adams talked about has
little importance since these extensive walls exist
throughout the search area. The thing that makes this
particular one different is the passageway that extended through it.

The Little Door

As remembered by Adams, the mining party rode
straight up to the long wall with no one seeing any

break whatsoever in the solid rock. Only by close examination could an opening be seen at all. The mouth of a narrow fissure was concealed behind a protruding, vertical column of stone. Once inside the unusual corridor, the riders discovered the long passageway cutting right through the bluff.

Although this sort of break or cut through a bluff does occur, it is rare. The Mexicans call it *un puerto* (a doorway). Adams named this one the Little Door, and now hundreds have searched for that unique doorway.

One other observation by Adams involved the irrigated Pumpkin Patch and the Long Bluff: Both were located on the elevated terrain of the mesa. Because of this, the bluff that so many searchers have tried to find can probably be seen for some distance. At the same time, the elevated mesa was apparently just a part of a general uplift. We know this because the route, after going through the Little Door, continued upward through a canyon in another ascension to still another elevated plateau. This plateau was the high ground from where most of the surrounding region would be observed.

The Haystacks

From this high mesa, the guide pointed out two mountain summits. They appeared to be about fifteen to twenty miles to the east, standing almost side by side. The guide referred to them as being the same two peaks they had seen from the White Mountain lookout. From that lookout, the miners had observed two distant points on a faraway horizon. Now, the two mountains were near at hand.

Who could say whether or not they were the same two? The guide may have been the only one who knew the answer to that question. It probably never occurred to the miners, who were too busy thinking about the gold. However, it is a question Adams must have pondered in later years when he was trying to relocate his lost bonanza, because even though he covered vast portions of New Mexico and Arizona, he never saw those two peaks again. If he had been able to locate them, he could probably have returned to the canyon of gold.

Adams said the two mountain peaks looked like haystacks in the late evening sun. They stood side by side, and they could easily be seen for a hundred miles from the White Mountain lookout.

When I first realized the implication of this combination of facts, I felt as if my efforts toward a closer understanding of the legend had compromised the story's credibility. According to the above description, by Adams himself, this two-peak landmark should be an easy thing to find. Yet, despite his years of searching and all of the miles covered, Adams simply never saw them again. Why?

The entire matter seemed to me to be a glaring contradiction to logic. Such a landmark ought to be easy to spot. But as I learned more about the legend—and about New Mexico—I came to realize that this strange contradiction was no more than one of the story's many hazy examples of a paradox. I also learned that strange contradictions, and hazy examples of paradox, can be something quite different when brought into the light of understanding.

As time went by, my interest in the two-peaked landmark grew. I became convinced that in his description of the double summits looking like haystacks, Adams was relaying one of the most important clues.

The Canyon of the Gold

After departing the high mesa, the party dropped down several hundred feet. They entered a canyon on what some writers described as a precarious trail. Once on the canyon's floor, the miners found springs and running water. They also found protected little meadows with tall grass for their horses. The men saw deer, rabbits, and other wild game. Adams said it was a beautiful place.

Because he spent many days and nights there, perhaps two weeks or longer, Adams' memory should have been accurate when it came to the detailed description of this canyon that he later gave repeatedly. That description was both colorful and graphic. He said that the only way into the canyon was over the trail they had come in on. All other access was blocked by sheer faces of rock hundreds of feet high.

Debris from landslides, fallen trees, and scattered boulders had effectively closed the downstream outlet; high vertical cliffs came together sealing the upstream end. The result was a canyon that was blocked at both ends. Adams described the valley between the blocked ends as something of a natural paradise.

Part of the reason Adams called this canyon a paradise can be found in the fact that he was there in the late summer and early autumn. That time of the year— in New Mexico—is the prime of the seasons. In the latter part of August and on into September, when these events were supposed to have taken place, there is little or no wind. The daytime temperatures are beginning to cool; the nights, while not yet cold, are just right for sleeping.

The miners were awakened each morning by the sound of birds singing their tribute to the new day. Scores of butterflies kept watch as the intruders washed out their gold, and, at that time of year, wildflowers turned the landscape into natural sprays of indescribable colors, kept clean and bright by afternoon showers.

While it lasted, they had camp fires and sunsets, the smell of venison cooking in the evening, and the sound of a rippling stream at night. It was a paradise. It was a golden Shangrila that only a few men have ever known.

First Indian Contact

Before the young guide left, he told the members of the expedition that the canyon was a campground of the Apaches. He also explained that the Indians could return at any time.

A few days passed, probably not more than two or three, before a big party of Indians appeared. Some accounts say these people were Apaches, others simply call them Indians. At any rate, they moved in and set up camp about three hundred yards below the miners. Adams said they were friendly enough. They told the miners they could stay for a while, as long as they kept their distance from the Indian camp. Then, for a few more days, the two parties got along well. The following quotation from the Byerts text describes the peaceful nature of this relationship.

> Up to this time there had been much friendship between the Indians and our party of miners, and it was very common for the children to be down in our camp . . . [5]

Byerts, of course, was quoting Adams and goes on to say that women were also a part of the Indian party.

The Indians and miners were neighbors for several days. Then, just as quickly as they had entered the canyon, the Indians were gone. They left at about the time the miners started work on their cabin. If the

Indians had thought of the mining camp as only a temporary thing, this construction represented something else again.

Adams always claimed it was Apaches who put on untimely end to the golden dream; he was there and he should have known. Here again, questions came into my mind. If they were Apaches, why did they not attack the Adams party in the beginning? The roving Apache bands were never famous for their congeniality, especially toward white miners.

In the Allen Account, Adams is said to have named the Apache chief Nana as leader of the band that attacked the miners. If that is true, then why the friendly attitude in the beginning, only to change so drastically in the end? I suppose it is possible that the Indians were merely waiting for the miners to split ranks when part of them would be going out for provisions. A well planned attack would then take out the miners, and yield up their provisions.

In one respect, this looks to be exactly what happened. On the other hand, this was a frail motive, and it was not the sort of thing that would have interested Chief Nana.

When it comes to motivation for the attacks, there are a number of possibilities. It could well have been something quite different than an Apache raid. In fact, the Apaches might not have had anything to do with this entire matter.

If not the Apaches, then who was it? There is one interesting possibility. When the mining party first came to the irrigated spot that Adams called the Pumpkin Patch, they had observed what they thought were Indian dwellings.

Throughout their history, Pueblo Indians have maintained irrigated farming plots as a part of their way of life. On the edge of such plots were constructed what was once known as *rancherias*. In addition to an allotment of land, each Indian farmer had a small shelter structure maintained for storage and for protection against the elements.

A few acres of irrigated fields with a number of shelter buildings could have been what the Adams party passed by. The irrigated farming plots and their rancherias had to be developed where water was easily obtainable. In some cases, this is known to have been many miles from the protection of the pueblo villages. Evidence of this can be found along the San Jose River, eastward from present-day Grants, where Acoma and Laguna farmers have used the water in the spring-fed river for centuries. In the past, there were other areas like this, due to a higher water table and a wetter climate.

Tensions between the Pueblo Indians and the roving nomadic tribes varied from time to time. During the more hostile periods, there was safety in numbers; at such times the pueblo offered the needed protection. There were also periods when the different tribes were at peace with one another. Then industrious Pueblo farmers developed the farming plots with the structures. Many adobe and rock house ruins throughout western New Mexico attest to this fact in places where surface water is now only a memory.

In the Byerts text, Adams is quoted as saying that the Pumpkin Patch was the first indication of farming they had seen since leaving the Pima villages. After they left the Pumpkin Patch, the mining party traveled on for another day's ride. That movement may have constituted a penetration into one of the pueblo domains. As in any domain, the natural resources found there belong to the keepers of the domain.

Gold Here—But More Over There!

Allen and Byerts, as well as others, have pointed to the fact that the Pima-Mexican guide claimed there was more gold, much more, over near the two haystack mountains. That location was still another day's ride from the canyon. If what the guide said was true, and at this point there remains little reason to doubt him, it means there were two places containing gold. It also means the two locations were a good distance from each other, possibly as much as twenty miles. This, in turn, would seem to indicate extensive accumulations of the precious metal.

According to Adams' recollection, the guide tried to tell the miners about coarser gold, and vastly more of it, at the final destination. The miners, however, would not leave the bonanza they had just found, and according to Adams, Davidson, and Brewer, it was just that, a bonanza. In the sand of the floor of the canyon, they found gold; they also found it in a ledge that was part of the highly mineralized canyon wall. While it was not as good as the canyon described by the guide, it was richer than anything the miners had ever run across. For them to go on to something else was out of the question.

Speculation regarding what might have been had the party continued to follow their guide has always run high among those who were interested in the Lost Adams. What the miners never did see will forever remain the guide's secret, until the day when these treasure troves are found and this entire mystery is understood.

How an occurrence of gold of this magnitude could have remained undiscovered throughout all of the years since this happening presents one of the intriguing questions about the American West. This is especially true in light of the tremendous effort by so many to find it.

In my own endeavor to understand, I have come to the conclusion that the gold may have been covered up. That covering action could have been the result of natural phenomenon, and it could have been due to human effort. I have not, however, completely ruled out the possibility that there is an unusual situation in which a canyon exists that is simply hidden away—a hidden canyon where no one ever goes.

AUTHOR'S ADVISORY:

In order for me to understand the frontier situation that existed in 1864, in the territories of New Mexico and Arizona, I determined that I should examine the history of the region. That history, I discovered, was a most interesting story about many different cultures and their connection with gold. My motivation, to begin with, was a search for answers that would tell me what actually happened to the Adams party, and why; but, being a history enthusiast, the further I delved into this unique and fascinating record of the Southwest, the more compelling it became to me. When I finished with this research, I came to the realization that for anyone, especially my readers, to have the information they need to fully understand the setting of the Lost Adams story, they must know something about this very turbulent civilization. The following chapter, New Mexico and Gold, is my attempt to provide that insight.

4

NEW MEXICO AND GOLD

While I began to dig deeper into the historical aspect of the story, I noticed that my favorite member of the opposite sex, my wife of more years than she likes to admit, was slowing falling victim to the same lure that had captured me. As her interest grew, she became an invaluable asset as a working partner in my research. Her name is Terry, and she is right there behind the *we's,* the *our's,* and the *I's* of this text.

In going over the various accounts of the massacres, I felt that the information left much to be desired. Some of this problem is the result of time and some of it must be attributed to Adams himself. I am not saying it did not happen as he described it, nevertheless, in my opinion, a number of questions are left unanswered.

For instance, why would an Apache band come into that canyon, set up camp, establish friendly terms with the miners, then leave, only to come back a few days later to kill them all in a barbaric ritual?

The whole idea of the massacres becomes even harder to understand when the responsibility for that action is given to the Apache chief, Nana. Adams said it was Nana; if that is true, it runs counter to most of the historical record concerning this chief. He would have killed them, all right, but that is not the point. It is the way Adams said it happened that produces the question.

The original pretext of friendship ending in tragic deception is hard to reconcile with Chief Nana's reputation. Most of his conflict with the white race was of a defensive nature. On other occasions, when he is known to have attacked, it was more often a matter of reprisal. According to Adams, the massacres were the result of unwarranted treachery.

Of course, it may have been that Adams simply never told the entire story, or perhaps he reported it inaccurately. For reasons of his own, he may have omitted telling about incidents that could have provided motivation for the attacks. It is just as possible that he was telling the story exactly as it happened, but in reality never knew himself what motivated the attacks or the identity of the attackers.

This line of thinking led us to the previously stated question. If not Apaches, then who were the raiders? Attempting to answer that proved to be a considerable undertaking in its own right. It took us to the local library in Grants, where Terry and I began the interesting process of searching for that answer.

Soon we realized that before we could even begin to understand what happened to the Adams expedition, we needed to develop an understanding of the various peoples who had existed in the region. This becomes something like looking at a faceted gemstone; each facet is important, but it is only by observing them all that the gem's true beauty can be appreciated.

This understanding begins with a clear look at the people who lived and died for hundreds of years in the mountains and on the deserts of the Southwest. Like any other civilization, there were times when the various factions disagreed and warred. The difference between their disagreements and ours, lies in the degree in which greed played a role.

In early times, disputes that were the result of jealousy over possessions came about more through necessity than through greed. The far-ranging nomadic tribes raided and killed each other and the sedentary Indians as well. To the nomads, it was a means of survival. It is doubtful that they could afford the extravagance of greed, a situation that has reversed itself in today's society.

In that day, the Pueblo Indians were scattered throughout New Mexico, up and down the valley of the Rio Grande and its tributaries, in much the same way as they are today. The most prized possession in the Southwest then, was turquoise. The people called it their *sky stone* because of its color. It was treasured and revered more than gold or silver and was used extensively in the production of jewelry. The sky-blue stone was combined with sea shells and coral that had been obtained through trade, and the resulting jewelry was but one of many artistic accomplishments.

The Pueblo Indians had a well developed society of people who lived in their own cities, in houses that were often four stories high. The architecture displayed in the construction of those Indian towns and cities represents a high degree of technical progress as did the highly developed irrigated farming operations they perfected.

They fashioned pots out of clay. From certain plants and rocks, they derived paints and dyes used in designs artistically applied to the pots—another work of art for which today's collectors pay handsomely. The Indians enjoyed arts and crafts; they farmed, hunted, and fished as a way of life and they survived, as had their ancestors before them.

There are old ruins in a great number of locations throughout New Mexico and its neighboring states.

With their numbers literally in the thousands, these ruins provide proof of the existence of one civilization after another for centuries. Some of those ruins, like Chaco Canyon, Bandelier, and Mesa Verde, were large population centers more than a thousand years ago. The sudden abandonment of those centers has never been fully understood. The Pueblo Indians of today and yesteryear also shared this tendency toward an urban society.

Their enemies were, as stated earlier, the nomadic Apache, Comanche, and Navajo bands. Although these bands were dangerous, they posed an even greater threat once they acquired horses from the Spanish. Horses, on the other hand, were a mixed blessing to the Pueblo inhabitants.

With the intrusion of the Spaniards came a general breakdown of that stable atmosphere and an increase of tension between the tribes. This worsening condition became a status quo for the next three hundred years.

The Spanish conquistadors brought with them the ages-old desire for conquest. They wanted vast territorial acquisitions, they wanted the mineral wealth of the regions they conquered, and they wanted the conversion of the native population to the Christian faith. The Spaniards wanted these three things, but their priorities were not necessarily in this exact order. Above all else, they wanted gold.

What this meant to the Indians was the beginning of the end of the self-determination they had always known. It signaled their deliverance to an enemy whose ways they did not understand, the subjugation of their numbers, and finally death and enslavement for many of them for generations to come. Such were the payments of conquest.

The first Spaniards to have a look at what was to become New Mexico are considered by most historians to be Cabeza de Vaca, Alonzo Maldonado, Andre

Dorantez, and his dark-skinned slave, Stephen Estevan. Their story, though unacceptable to some, has become a part of history.

That story recalls the voyage of a party of Spanish colonists attempting to cross the Gulf of Mexico. The crossing ended in a disastrous shipwreck on the gulf coast, near the present site of Galveston, Texas. These four survived and were taken prisoner by local Indians.

After living with these people for a time, the four Spaniards escaped. Their route took them across southwestern Texas and into New Mexico. The extent of their far-reaching adventure into what is now known as New Mexico is a matter of contention among historians. Some believe that only the southeastern corner was crossed, while others argue that, in their year-long walk, the four Spaniards crossed two rivers, the Pecos and the Rio Grande.

The four told of encountering many aboriginal tribes, some of whom lived in walled cities of stone and plaster construction. The Spaniards also claimed that some of the inhabitants of the strange cities spoke of gold, silver, and other metals. When they told their story in the Spanish settlements of Mexico, it created a great deal of interest. The journey of these four took place in 1535 and 1536, and as a direct result of their reports, another exploratory expedition was formed.

In 1538, Antonio de Mendoza, then Viceroy of Mexico, used the talents of Friar Marcos de Niza (who had risen to become chief of the Franciscan Friars who were slated for missionary work on the new northern frontier) and the Negro slave Stephen Estevan for a reconnaissance into the far northern regions. The two were to gain information about the native people and their cities of wealth and gold of which Cabeza de Vaca had spoken.

This expedition, though small in comparison to later parties, resulted in some important developments.

The first, and perhaps the most important of these developments, was the fact that this was the first effort in the long and colorful story of the Spanish conquest of the southwestern part of the United States. Because of this effort, the Indian inhabitants of what would some-day be called Arizona were introduced to two races of mankind that they had never known before.

The Spanish party was well received as it traveled northward out of Mexico. That good reception continued until Estevan, with an advanced group, entered an area near the Pueblo then known as Cibola (Zuni). There, after making excessive demands of the Zuni people, Estevan was killed.

Friar Niza, upon being told of Estevan's death by execution, reluctantly advanced to within sight of the Indian city of Cibola. He made some observations and then turned back toward Mexico. At that time, most of the Mexico Indians who had been with Estevan were released by the Zunis, and they joined Niza in his exodus. A few young men were detained by the Zunis, and at least one of these was still there when the pueblo was visited by Coronado a year later.

In the reports of his journey, Friar Marcos de Niza, like Cabeza de Vaca before him, told of seeing a civilization of people who were industrious, advanced, and who possessed gold. His description of the Cibola Pueblo, which he had seen from a distance, was a confirmation of reports he claimed to have received from natives as his party originally moved northward.

In effect, he told of seeing an Indian city of many houses and buildings that were constructed of masonry and stone. The people wore clothing made of cotton and ornaments of turquoise. They were successful agriculturalists who ate well and lived better than other tribes the friar had observed.

Some of the natives he had talked to before reaching Cibola, told Niza that the pueblo was one of seven cities that lay eastward toward a great river. Those same native sources also disclosed the fact that the inhabitants of the seven cities were indeed the possessors of gold.

Viceroy Mendoza, acting on the reports by Friar Niza, set in motion the machinery to create the vast expedition led by Coronado. In the spring of 1540 that expedition became a reality. Coronado, with Friar Marcos de Niza in charge of the Franciscan order, together with some three hundred Spaniards, and nearly a thousand Indian guides, servants, and laborers, began one of the most famous and historical adventures of all time.

The large, cumbersome operation moved slowly. It took many months to put Mexico behind them and penetrate what later became the United States.

There was something of a change in the attitude of the natives of the region that is now eastern Arizona. That change was a noticeable departure from the outgoing friendliness Friar Marcos had benefitted from the year before. Upon inquiry, it was learned that the residents of Cibola had requested that their neighbors to the southwest stop the advancing Spaniards any way they could. From this, it would appear that the Zuni hatred of Estevan, a result of his conflict with them, was still fresh in their minds.

We know, of course, that Coronado was not deterred; it was only a matter of time before his massive force stood at the threshold of their city. Once more fighting and conflict erupted, and this time many Indians died. This was only the first of many skirmishes as the proud pueblo people resisted the beginning of Spanish encroachment.

The power of Coronado moved like a fever through the land. As the expedition progressed, the natives learned about God from the Catholic friars; that is, they learned about God after their submission to the often cruel authority of the conquistadors. Strangely, the Indians knew of no gold.

If success can be measured by an ability to get along with the natives, Friar Marcos de Niza was one of the most successful of those early Spanish explorers. His reasons for going into the northern country were not based on greed. He was concerned about the souls of the people, not how much gold they possessed.

Because of the difference in motivation and the results thereof, Coronado and his officers became outraged at Niza. Matters only worsened when the wealthy kingdoms he had spoken of were not found. They accused the friar of deception and lying, accusations that were once directed at Christ himself. Eventually, the conquistador sent Friar Niza back to Mexico.

Coronado continued his exploitation of the pueblos. His explorations extended even beyond the pueblos into vast portions of what was to become Arizona, New Mexico, Texas, and Kansas. The quest for gold never let up.

The tremendous effort put forth by the people of this expedition ultimately produced preliminary maps of the areas involved but precious little gold. Coronado came for gold, and gold was also what motivated most of the Spaniards who were with him. That is the only realistic conclusion when one considers the events of the preceding years in Mexico.

In less than fifty years, Spain had discovered a new world; in the process, her explorers had found some of the richest accumulations of gold on earth. The success of Cortez was the envy of virtually every able-bodied man in both Spain and Mexico, all of them, that is, except the Indians.

The new world representative of the Spanish crown was, as already pointed out, Viceroy Mendoza. The treatment of the aboriginal people had become important to the viceroy; he did not want the mistakes of the past repeated. Therefore, when license was granted to the conquistadors for their exploration and colonizing expeditions, the treatment of the native population became an important consideration.

Policy, however, is one thing; the application of that policy is another. Coronado's first responsibility was to the people of his party and their safety. And when one group forces its will on another, for whatever reason, there will be conflict.

It may well be that the exertion of power and the quest for riches displayed by Estevan and Coronado became the very things that destroyed any chance for good relations or finding gold.

The story of the mistakes made by the Aztec and the Inca people in the offering of gold as an appeasement to the Spaniards was no doubt carried to the northern inhabitants by the Indian servants who were with both Estevan and Coronado. Their doing so planted the seeds of mistrust and suspicion that plagued the Spanish conquistadors from then on.

One further point of observation concerning the Coronado expedition was the correlation of the routes that were taken by Coronado and the Adams party. Both involved the Gila River, the area that is now the site of Springerville, Arizona, and the same part of west-central New Mexico. Perhaps if Adams' young guide had led Coronado, our Southwest might have developed differently.

It is a fact of history that routes taken by the various exploratory trips of the Coronado expedition came close to the rich mining districts that were later developed. Coronado missed them and so did a lot of other people.

In the remaining half of the sixteenth century, other Spanish parties entered the *new* Mexico. None of them, however, could be compared with the Coronado expedition. Then, in 1598, the situation changed.

Oñate's Signature at El Morro, April 16, 1605. This Was 15 Years Before the Pilgrims Landed at Plymouth Rock.

Don Juan de Oñate, another conquistador, crossed the Rio Grande in the area now occupied by El Paso, Texas. With him came some four hundred soldiers, Franciscan priests, and colonists, together with their families and Indian servants.

Except for the Indian servants and the direction in which the party was moving, they must have resembled the American pioneers of the nineteenth century. They came on horseback, driving herds of cattle, sheep, and horses; they came in covered wagons with, in most cases, all of their worldly possessions; they came to colonize and claim the new land for Spain.

Within two years, Oñate had established the first provincial capital of the new Spanish province. This center of Spanish power was located near the old Indian

El Morro National Monument
Out in western New Mexico, along the "ANCIENT WAY," there is a place called El Morro. The Spanish name means "the headland" or "the bluff." At the base of this great bluff of sandstone rock lies a natural pool of clear blue water. This eternal pool is maintained entirely by melting winter snow and summer rainfall. It provided critically needed water for travelers in this region from the time of Coronado onward through much of the 19th century. Starting with the Spanish conquistador Oñate, visitors here left their names forever etched in the sandstone walls of El Morro.

pueblo of San Juan. It was close to the juncture of the
Rio Grande and the Chama rivers and only a few miles
north of the present city of Española. In less than twenty years, this capital moved to a permanent home in
Santa Fe.

One of Oñate's first priorities was the disbursement
of the Franciscan missionaries to the various pueblos.
Once again, disagreement with Spanish policies erupted
into conflict, and again the result was brutal treatment
of the natives.

From the outset of Oñate's arrival, some of the
tribes were at odds with the conquistador. The people of
Acoma were no exception. Trouble developed at the
Acoma Pueblo when a small party of Spaniards, under
the command of one of Oñate's captains, was attacked
and some Spaniards were killed. That skirmish brought
a reprisal from the conquistador. A bloody battle resulted and when it was over, hundreds of Acomas lay dead.
The once proud City in the Sky[1] was burned out and literally reduced to rubble.

The Acoma Pueblo was built on top of a high mesa
as a means of defense. For centuries the tactic was successful. The high fortress commanded the name City in
the Sky for the Native Americans of that day.

By Oñate's decree, most of the Acoma survivors
were sentenced to twenty years of personal servitude. In
addition, all Acoma males over the age of twenty-five
had one foot cut off.

Two Hopi Indians who were at Acoma at the time,
and had fought and been captured, had their right
hands taken off. Then, the pair was released to go home.
This was done as an example to other Indians of the resolution of the conquistador.

For a period of time, the Acoma people were scattered. Some of them were sent to Mexico, others were
distributed among other pueblos.

Three decades later, under the direction of the Acomas' first permanent priest, Friar Juan Ramirez, the restoration of the City in the Sky began. This man, like Friar Marcos de Niza, was successful in his dealings with the Indian people. History tells us that his success came as a result of his ability to give of himself to the needs of the Acomas, and in this restoration, their needs were great.

Examples such as this were altogether too few among the ranks of the Spaniards. With those early Spanish operations, however, the tendency was not toward giving; it was toward taking, demanding, and force. Unfortunately, this attitude also extended to many of the Catholic missionaries and the way they approached their work.

Consequently, the Indians, though partially converted to believe in the Catholic doctrine, had no illusions concerning the Spanish. In 1680, the Indians revolted and drove the Spaniards back to the El Paso area, all but out of what is now New Mexico. In the strongest unification ever known, the pueblos came together to form an alliance against the Spaniards in an attempt to annihilate the entire Spanish population. It was their purpose to kill every man, woman, and child.

Fortunately for the Spaniards, some of the converted Indians gave early warnings and in so doing, they lessened the death toll to a degree. Still, hundreds died before the final pullout.

As for the reasons behind the revolution, the early Spanish writers wrote that it was a reaction to religious oppression. They said the missionaries demanded total abandonment of native beliefs and practices. This demand was backed up by military force to the point of slavery, torture, and even death.

Time after time in the studies of this era, much use was made of the word *servitude*. When this occurs, it often alludes to the use of women and children in the homes of the colonists as domestics. When Indian males are mentioned, it speaks of them as working in fields or workshops. They are almost never discussed in connection with mining operations. This is understandable when one takes into consideration the source of most of the historical record—early Spanish chroniclers who were writing about the activities of the new province to the viceroy in Mexico City or to the royal court in Spain.

From the beginning of Spain's interest in the vast northern frontier, the viceroys responsible for the exploration and colonizing expeditions were concerned about the welfare of the aboriginal people. It was because of just such concerns that Oñate was brought up on charges, in connection with the assault on Acoma.

Hearings were held in which he was made to account for his actions; he did face penalties. With this in mind, it is not hard to believe that there were certain operations that were never written about, at least not in the above mentioned reports.

Although few and scattered, other accounts tell of early Spanish mining and of great sacrifices made by enslaved Indians. Both gold and silver, in terms of millions of dollars, were reported to have been removed by the Spaniards in this virtually forgotten industry.

Most historians have little or nothing to say on this subject. One of the reasons for this is that so little is known, and that is mostly because of the 1680 Indian revolution. The following quoted material on this subject is from one of the most respected of the historians, Hubert Howe Bancroft.

> The history of this province, from the fall of Acoma in 1599 to the great revolt of 1680, can never be made complete, for lack of data. The home archives were destroyed in the revolt, and we must depend on such fragments as found their way out into the world before that outbreak.[2]

Eighty years is a long time. With only fragments of information by which to judge it, who can say what really happened then?

From the time of Coronado until the revolt of 1680, the Indians had endured 140 years of on-again, off-again Spanish domination. As I read those old records, the one thing that impressed me most was how little anyone had gained. Perhaps the Spaniards had been able to mine some minerals. Just how much will never be known for sure. Whatever their success along that line, it was *not* with the willing help of the Indians. There is every reason to believe that just the opposite was true.

The Spanish pullout was little more than a run for their lives. In mid-August of 1680, after withstanding several days of siege, they began their withdrawal from New Mexico. Behind them, the Spanish left almost four hundred of their number dead. Comprising that number were men, women, and children, brutally slaughtered in an almost simultaneous set of massacres that took place in all but a few of the pueblos. This kind of hatred is not easily explained.

In the wake of the Spanish withdrawal, the Indians destroyed not only their records but everything Spanish. Spanish buildings were burned, in some cases leveled to the ground. All forms of religious paraphernalia were eliminated. The destruction did not stop there.

They went to the mines, and proceeded to fill them in. The Indians were meticulous in this cover-up, carefully removing all traces of the mines so that the metals would never again bring hardship upon them. The success of the Indians in this cover-up can be measured by the fact that future Spaniards would not be the harvesters of any great volume of gold and silver in New Mexico.

Although the covering of the old mines and the obliteration of the trails that led to them was successful, one piece of evidence was not eliminated. Today, remains of old Spanish smelters can still be found, scattered all the way from the Taos area in the north to the mountainous terrain around Socorro in the south. In the not-too-distant past, many of these timeless relics yielded slag that contained surprising amounts of gold and silver.[3]

For twelve years, the Indians had their freedom. It was not, however, what they could call their shining hour. Popé, the San Juan Indian who was the leader of the revolution, became obsessed with power and proved to be no better as a ruler than the Spaniards he had dispossessed. His abusive and oppressive reign ended in another revolutionary war, this time between some of the pueblos.

Adding to the misery of the people were several years of severe drought. Winters became extremely mild with little or no snowfall in the northern mountains. Without the normal summer rains, the water tables dropped, causing creeks and springs to become arid wastes that in turn dried up the Rio Grande.

A combination of these disagreeable factors (for the Native American population) could only have made it easier for the intrusion of the next Spanish conquistador. There had been other parties, mostly small and reconnaissance in nature, during the preceding years and now, a larger company was coming to reclaim the territory for the King of Spain.

In 1692, Don Diego de Vargas led an expedition of reconquest up the Rio Grande. The first of many diplomatic victories by de Vargas took place as the Spaniards reclaimed their old villa at Santa Fe. In the next three months, pueblo after pueblo came back under Spanish rule, and did so without the shedding of blood.

The credit for this bloodless campaign belongs to de Vargas and his unique powers of persuasion. His retaking of the villa of Santa Fe is still celebrated in the annual festivities of the Santa Fe Fiesta. Unfortunately, his recolonizing efforts in the years following the reconquest did meet with opposition. From 1693 through 1696, that opposition became the cause of many battles.

In time, all of the pueblos did capitulate. Acoma, the newly founded Laguna, and the Zuni pueblos were among the last to accept the Spanish authority. The Acomas gave their oath of allegiance to Spain, reciting the Spanish Act of Obedience, in the summer of 1699.

The next hundred years were almost a repeat of the first eighty years of the century just completed under Spanish rule. One possible exception was a reduced emphasis on mining. Although occasional uprisings occurred, there were no more successful Indian revolutions.

During the early years of the eighteenth century, the pueblos returned to a passive existence, marked by Spanish oppression and pressure from the ever dangerous nomadic tribes. Indeed, all of the non-nomadic tribes were trapped into that passive existence. The Apaches, after having perfected their skills in the equestrian arts, became an even fiercer enemy. Then, in the latter half of the century, the Navajos, Comanches, and Utes, having also acquired horses, became formidable foes as well.

The Spanish population grew slowly, and Mexicans began to migrate as part of the Spanish colonizing effort. Both faced the growing problem of the raiding renegade tribes.

Perhaps the only real progress made by the Spaniards throughout that entire century were the accomplishments of the Franciscan priests. Many Catholic missions built or restored during the eighteenth century are still in use today. The message that is taught in those missions now is the same that was taught then. It had a conciliating effect on those who would listen and thus affected the civilization that then existed. It gave the many different cultures a common ground of understanding, just as it does today.

Once more, the records that were kept say little about mining. It is almost as though the Spaniards forgot about gold, though that is not likely. Some mining was carried on. Gold was produced at Tiro, in the Cerrillos district. A few other locations were named, but the efforts by the industry during this period merely resulted in a low profile on the subject.

By the end of the eighteenth century, the Spanish population had risen to only a little over 23,000. That is not much growth for 260 years of colonizing effort. Possibly this fact, more than any other, points out the extreme hardships suffered by the Spaniards as they fought everything from belligerent Indians to harsh winters—at times to the point of starvation—in their efforts to colonize this new land.

Throughout the early years of the nineteenth century, the Spaniards and Mexicans allied themselves with some of the pueblo tribes in mutual defense against the devastating forays of Navajo and Apache raiders.

During the period 1811–1821, Mexico waged its war of independence from Spain. The war had little effect on the northern province, however, and the population there simply awaited the outcome.

The end of Spanish rule came in the closing months of 1821. The establishment of Mexican authority, in Santa Fe, provided a more relaxed atmosphere for the opening of trade lanes with the United States. Then the traders came, and in their wake was created the Santa Fe Trail.

In 1828, only seven years after Spain relinquished its control of the former province, prospectors rediscovered the Old Placers gold district (of early Spanish mining) in the Ortiz Mountains between Albuquerque and Santa Fe. This discovery increased traffic along the Santa Fe Trail, further escalating its importance as a frontier access.

The gold brought many Americans into the Mexican province, thus creating the first American interest in New Mexico's gold. That interest saw the discovery of a score of gold-producing districts within the next fifty years in New Mexico alone. In light of the acknowledged Spanish gold production of nearly three hundred years, one might call this phenomenal.

In 1839, another major gold strike occurred near the present town of Golden. Called the New Placers, the discovery was several miles south of the Old Placers strike. By 1845, production from the two areas was valued in terms of hundreds of thousands of dollars (millions by today's standards) for the year. The little town of Golden, called Tuerto at that time, set population records, thereby becoming a charter member in the community of western boom towns.

By 1846, steadily deteriorating relations between the U.S. and Mexico resulted in the Mexican-American War. The root of the problem between the two countries lay firmly planted in disputes created by the U.S. annexation of Texas. Accordingly, with boundary claims of both Mexico and the United States at the heart of the question, this war, like the war for Mexican Independence, had little effect on the people along the Rio Grande.

General Stephen Watts Kearny, commanding an army column, entered New Mexico in August 1846. Meeting no resistance, he led his troops on to Santa Fe, where he lost no time raising the Stars and Stripes, and in proclaiming the former Mexican department to be under the provisional authority of the United States.

The original construction of Fort Marcy, the first American fort in New Mexico, was begun within a matter of days following Kearny's arrival in Santa Fe. In the course of the next ten years, several forts were built.Of particular concern were the Navajos. Their population had doubled over that of the Apaches, and their raids were increasing dramatically.

Between 1850 and 1860, the Navajos became a ruthless people. Their depredations were directed against not only their old enemies but the American population as well. It was as though they considered themselves invincible. They started having problems with their Apache neighbors, on the south and the Utes on the north. Finally, the intense hatred of the Navajos by everyone in the region began taking its toll.

Military sorties, originated by the Spaniards were continued by the Mexican-Indian militia and later by the U.S. Army. In time, those forces, under the command of Colonel Kit Carson, supplied the answer to the Navajo problem.

In the first week of January 1864, Colonel Carson and nearly four hundred men began a systematic round up of the Navajo tribe. The U.S. government had decided that the only real solution was to rout the Indians from their fortress in Canyon de Chelly and other strongholds in what they considered their homeland, and to move the entire population to a small reservation in eastern New Mexico. The operation took many months, but by the end of summer, some seven thousand Navajo men, women, and children had completed a rigorous three hundred mile walk to the Bosque Redondo Reservation.

That reservation was near Fort Sumner where the topography of the country was a dramatic change for the Navajo. The beautiful mountain areas they had always known were left far behind, replaced by flatlands and sage-covered prairies.

Part of their "long walk" (as it came to be known) took the Navajos near the pueblo villages of former adversaries. There can be little doubt that the residents of Acoma and Laguna were relieved to see their old enemies in such a subdued state as they walked along under the watchful eyes of the cavalry.

It is also possible, even highly probable, that Pueblo Indians observing this vast movement of humanity were seeing something else. If they looked hard at all, they could see a change taking place in the balance of power. Changes in power had occurred before, as with other tribes, with the Spaniards, and the Mexicans, but this was different. In less than a score of years, the Americans had displayed more power than any of the previous cultures. The aspect of such power was probably more than just a little disturbing in the minds of those observers.

Some Navajos did not make the "long walk." In the process of being rounded up, several families escaped and made their way south and east to an isolated area on what is now known as the Rio Salado River. There, near a great spring, these people created their own civilization. They were the ancestors of the Alamo Indians, also called the Puertocitos, a division of the Navajo Tribe to this day.

To say that the people who escaped Carson's roundup were the only Navajos to make the Rio Salado location their home might be inaccurate There are accounts that a few Navajos were already there and that others, escaping the forced march, had joined them.

At times the Alamo Navajos were mistaken for Apaches, as their wearing apparel closely resembled that of their nomadic brothers. In addition to this, the area in which they settled along the Rio Salado River was on a trail that the Apaches had used for centuries. The Apaches had made frequent use of the great spring these Navajos came to call their own, Alamo Springs. Indeed, in 1864, both tribes were there to some degree; both Navajos and Apaches were along the Rio Salado River, along that *northern county line of Socorro County*. And not far away were Acomas, Lagunas, and other Indian factions.

Overshadowing the events that were occurring in New Mexico were those historic and tragic clashes of the Civil War. While the Adams party was mining its gold in that secret canyon, Atlanta, Georgia, was falling to Union forces.

In the closing months of this most unusual year, 1864, General William Tecumseh Sherman, in a strategic move designed to split the Confederacy, began an offensive that ultimately resulted in his notorious march to the sea. In Washington, a war-weary President Abraham Lincoln longed for the day the conflict would end. He was to see that day—and only five more.

As we know, prejudice and hatred did not end with the Emancipation Proclamation; they were a part of life in the Southwest and even more so in New Mexico. There were so many different factions of people involved and, to some degree, all hated one another. This was that status quo that had existed for three hundred years.

The old problems: Indian against Indian and Indian against the Spanish and Mexican colonist were finally resolved by the new power that was moving through the land. The Americans used men like Kearny and Carson and others like them. A great many human beings, from all of the various factions, gave up their lives in the forty-year conflict called the Indian Wars.

The year 1864 was the midway point in the American offensive effort, and it was also the year most filled with violence and hatred. Such was the ultimate result, when tribe after tribe came to terms with the U.S. Army. History tells us that the American strength was not a matter of numbers because most of the forts established during this period were not strongly garrisoned. In fact, for over thirty years following the building of the first fort at Santa Fe, many forts were built and operated for a time, only to have their garrisons transferred to another location.

During the first half of the 1860s, the Civil War had its effect on the garrisons of those New Mexico forts; much of the military's manpower was used up in that conflict. Events that did happen on that western frontier came about because of an extraordinary effort by those who were there. They had their hands full through those bitter years of struggle and turmoil.

Because of such turmoil the hatred of white Americans by various Indian factions reached its peak in 1864. Of course, many of the pueblos held no particular animosity toward the whites, but there can be little doubt that even they viewed the American intrusion with some degree of frustration.

This was the situation the Adams party rode into. It was a hornet's nest, filled with passion, anguish, and death. It was a point in time when the rules of justice came under the dictates of the one rule—survival of the fittest.

Did they know what they were doing? Were they aware of the dangers involved? If they had known, would they have gone in anyway? The answer to all three questions is probably yes. The miners knew risks were involved in such an undertaking, but they lusted after gold, and gold made the risks worth taking.

This was the story of New Mexico, the story that Terry and I came to know as we tried to answer the question about those who attacked the miners. From our study, it became evident that in 1864 many tribes regarded the whites as their enemy, while others feared the strength of the U.S. Army. Some tribes that had suffered through hundreds of years of oppression had deep-seated roots of fear when it came to any intruding power.

In effect, we came to realize that any of the various factions could have perpetrated those attacks. To some degree, they all had the motivation.

The story of New Mexico held a number of interesting episodes for Terry and me. Coronado's exploration of the very area where we now live was fascinating in itself. He and those who were with him really expected to find the Seven Cities of Cibola, seven cities where the Indian people wore trinkets of gold. Variations of that expectation continued in the minds of the Spanish people for many generations. I could not help wondering: Why?

Even when one expedition after another came into this region and reported little or no success in discovering gold, the Spaniards persisted in their efforts. They continued to try for three hundred years. Indeed, according to historians, the Spaniards were almost a failure at finding gold in significant amounts in what is now the United States.

Then within just a few years of Spain's exodus, Mexican and American prospectors found gold all across New Mexico and what became Arizona and California. It is also historical fact that since that first discovery in 1828, gold has been mined in virtually *every* mountain range in New Mexico.

The four survivors of the Cabeza de Vaca party were the first Spaniards to touch this part of the Southwest. They returned to Mexico with a story related to them by Indians about other Indians with gold. These four men were not a threat to the people with whom they came into contact during their adventure. The man of God, Friar Marcos de Niza, was not a threat, and he heard the same stories about Indians with gold.

Then, there was Estevan. He was a Spaniard and he was a threat. In truth, Estevan was much more than that. He was an example of others who would follow him. He was black-skinned, and he talked about white-skinned men who were following him. In these things, Estevan was a mystery, something the people of Cibola did not understand.

The historians report that Estevan was demanding and aggressive and that made him the object of further apprehension. It is human nature to fear what we do not understand, especially when aggression is part of that misunderstanding. Estevan quickly became an enemy to the natives of Cibola and they dealt with him accordingly.

The story of the Spanish conquest of the Aztec civilization in Mexico, as well as the story of the Spaniards' love of gold, was doubtlessly transmitted to the people of Cibola by those of Estevan's party who were detained. Such news was certainly cause for alarm and the development of fear. With that fear having a year to ferment, the resulting conflict with Coronado was nothing more than a predictable inevitability.

By the time the Coronado expedition reached Cibola, there is a good chance that any gold belonging to the natives between there and the Rio Grande River was well hidden. Such an action, however large or small (if it did happen), could have been the beginning of a cover-up that would continue for centuries. There was little to encourage trust between the Spanish and the Pueblo Indians throughout those times.

Before leaving this subject, I would like to add a further word regarding the similarities between the Adams party and the Coronado expedition. We found it quite a coincidence that these two operations, a little over three hundred years apart, were both motivated by the word of Indians who were telling essentially the same story about unusual amounts of gold in what appears to be the same part of western New Mexico.

In constructing the cabin, the miners may have unknowingly stirred a basic trepidation in the Indians who attacked them, a fear shared by generation after generation of a society of people sitting on top of a hoard of metal, probably thought by them to have come out of the pits of hell itself.

As a result of my attempt to understand the collective failures of Adams, Shaw, Brewer, and the many who followed them, I began to believe more and more that a place does exist in New Mexico that few people have ever seen. This obscure place would have the capacity to conceal all of the major landmarks lying near the strike that Adams had talked about.

From that out-of-the-way place, one man had once walked to the Rio Grande River in less than a week; other men had gone by horseback to Fort Wingate—in only four days.

5

THE SEARCHERS

While the historical record of nineteenth century New Mexico and Arizona territories is a story of cultural collision and war, it is also the story of gold and those who searched for it. After the major strikes in California in 1849, prospecting and mining became the two main thrusts of an industry that was second to none between the Rocky Mountains and the Pacific Ocean.

Despite the fact that a virtual state of war existed between some of the Indian tribes and the steadily advancing tide of white men, expeditions continued to be launched in a search for precious metals. The struggle between the frontiersmen and their Native American enemies became so intense that, at one point in the 1860s, it threatened to shut down prospecting and mining completely.

One of the results of the hostility was the organization of both civilian and military operations, whose purpose was to seek out the belligerent Indian bands and bring them under control. At the head of the military part of this project was General James H. Carleton. He devised a plan and requested help from the governors of both Sonora and Chihuahua provinces in Mexico, as well as from Governor Goodwin of the Arizona Territory, in an effort to force the Indians to live in peace.

One of the largest citizen expeditions of this joint effort was led by King S. Woolsey.[1] In the early months of 1864, Woolsey managed to put together a force of about a hundred men, mostly ex-soldiers and prospectors. Although they did some prospecting for metals, their main function was to find and harass bands of hostile Indians. This operation took place in Apache areas in Arizona. Similar groups were formed in other localities.

Several of the mountain peaks, rivers, and canyons were named during such trips; in many cases, the names are still in use today. Additionally, early maps were drawn, definite trails were established, and a little gold was found.

On the military side of this endeavor, Colonel Kit Carson (as stated in Chapter 4) carried out his orders in the relocation of the Navajo Tribe, and other units of the cavalry rounded up some four hundred Apaches. This was all part of the program to bring the Indians to terms. Most of these events took place during that very turbulent year—1864.

One possible benefit of this unusual effort—beneficial, that is, for the Adams expedition—was the cooling effect it had on the Indians as a whole. It steered them away from large parties of whites and caused them to behave in a cautious manner. Perhaps this explains why Adams and his long column of riders were able to cross so much of Apacheria without being attacked.

Then too, not all Apaches were hostile. A good deal of the Adams party's route was through White Mountain Apache territory, and most of that tribe was less aggressive than some of its neighbors.

Many of the mining districts that did come into being were originally founded by the adventurous prospectors of that day. Some paid the ultimate price so that others could develop an industry. A few, like those in the Adams party, died a senseless and terrifying death and left as their only legacy the lost gold of what might have been the greatest find of them all. Found somewhere in the wake of those old traditions are—the searchers.

Of the many who joined Adams in his efforts to return to his great strike, one man's loyalty to the endeavor continued long after Adams died. That man was Captain C. A. Shaw. He had once been the captain of a merchant ship, and the title had stayed with him on the deserts of the Southwest, where he eventually became interested in the mining game. After meeting Adams, Shaw became the first in a long line of searchers.

Virtually everyone who had anything to do with this story's beginning gave Captain Shaw high marks when it came to such things as integrity and a sense of responsibility. In fact, during my extensive researching of the legend, I never read a negative word about him. Having mastered a ship put him in a unique class. He was not only respected as a man among men, but he in turn would have known the difference between men of honor and the bilge rats that always infiltrate society. Captain Shaw had total faith in Adams.

His searching began in the 1870s with Adams and continued until 1910 when he simply grew too old to meet the rigorous demands of the quest. The captain touched the lives of many throughout those years and he became an inspiration to all who knew him. The combination of Adams and Shaw, and the type of men they were, gave the legend the credibility it needed to endure.

As Adams had picked his searching partner carefully, so did Captain Shaw. When Adams died of a heart

attack, Shaw went looking for a man who had a reputation for honesty, knew the country of western New
Mexico, and was acquainted with prospecting and mining. He found these qualities in the person of Langford
Johnston, who at that time was running a cattle operation near Alma, New Mexico.

Once more, a solid bond was formed between two
well-respected men. That bond lasted for a quarter of a
century and took these two over thousands of miles
together. If there was a quality more representative of
the type of men they were, beyond being respected by
their peers, it was surely their dedication to finding the
mine that Adams had once seen. For Langford Johnston,
it became a lifetime involvement, just as it was for Shaw
and Adams before him.

The searching accomplished by Shaw and Johnston
included portions of the Mogollon Mountains east of
Alma and areas to the northwest of Socorro, New
Mexico. They also traveled through the mesa country to
the east and north of Springerville, Arizona. The
endeavor became the central interest in their lives; it
claimed not only their energies, and literally years out of
those lives, but much of their personal fortunes as well.

In judging their failure to find the lost mine, one
must always take into consideration the immensity of
the region in which they conducted their search—and
the time frame in which that searching took place.

Along with Langford Johnston, several other men
also took up the quest at the side of Captain Shaw. One
of these was the writer of the previously mentioned
newspaper article, W. H. Byerts of Socorro. Byerts had
first heard the story of the Lost Adams in the early
1880s. He later met Captain Shaw and became deeply
interested in Shaw's efforts to find the old mine. Byerts
also became acquainted with several of the men who
had worked with Adams. From these sources Byerts
gathered the information in his pamphlet.

Charles Allen was another man who became interested in the captain's search and went with him on many of his trips. Allen, like Byerts, wrote the story down in his own text, *The Adams Diggings Story.*[2] The two accounts are much alike in most important details, but they were written by two different men who had access to different sources of information. In their writings, both men displayed an unquestioning faith in Captain Shaw; both wrote of Shaw's absolute belief in Adams.

In his experience with Shaw, and also as a result of his independent efforts, Charles Allen met and talked to people throughout much of Arizona and New Mexico in his own quest for knowledge about this story. He did this over a period of time starting in the 1880s and continuing into the 1930s.

Among those he came to know was the man named Kirkpatrick who was discussed earlier in this text as having been at Fort Whipple in 1864. According to the Allen Account, survivor, Jack Davidson was taken to Fort Whipple by the party of scouts who found the two survivors wandering in the White Mountains.

Kirkpatrick became friendly with Davidson during his stay at Fort Whipple, and Davidson related the details of the gold venture to him, including the subsequent massacres that had left all dead except himself and one other man, Adams. Allen learned this story from Kirkpatrick several years later and found it to be a collaboration of the Adams revelation.

As a result of conversations he had with Kirkpatrick, there can be little doubt that Charles Allen made good use of the story that was first told by Davidson. This special insight would only have strengthened the Allen Account.

Both Allen and Byerts did a fine job of laying out the various facts about the old tradition. In substance, however, they did much more than that. They tell us the

story of those early searchers who were completely con-
sumed in the effort of trying to find that old discovery
after its location had been swallowed up by time and cir-
cumstance.

In retrospect, we should remember that when this
event—and the original searches that followed it—took
place, it was a period filled with many tales of gold and
silver strikes. It says something when so many individ-
uals of that era put forth the kind of effort they did in
attempting to locate the Lost Adams. That was a big
part of the story of those two accounts and of hundreds
of others since then.

Still another man who became part of Captain
Shaw's effort was A. M. Tenney, Jr. His story, in connec-
tion with John Brewer, is given in the chapter, "The
Survivors." Before John Brewer became involved with
Tenney, Captain Shaw paid him a visit in the mid-1880s.

Captain Shaw had come to Round Valley (now
Springerville) in an attempt to establish the trail that
was once followed by Adams and himself. Several years
before, the two of them had been there together, trying
to relocate the route of the original mining expedition.

According to Tenney, he, Captain Shaw, and others
in the Shaw party made a number of trips around the
area. On one occasion, they went up to a divide in the
White Mountains looking for an unusual pine tree that,
after coming out of the ground, had grown horizontally
for several feet before once more becoming vertical.
Shaw said it looked like a horse, and that after a shower, they had used the tree to lay clothing on to dry.

According to Adams this tree was on the original
trail and pointed out its further course. Tenney said they
were never able to find the unusual tree, but explained
that some of this area had been the scene of forest fires
in recent years and that the tree may simply have
burned.

A few days later, with Tenney as their guide, the Shaw party went east of the Little Colorado River (where the Tenney farm was located) into some rough country composed of mesas, and cedar-covered hills. Once more, Captain Shaw was unable to identify any of the landmarks they saw. After spending several days at this, they returned to the Tenney farm.

From there, the Shaw group, minus Tenney, moved north toward present day St. Johns; then turned east once again. Some time later, Tenney talked to their guide who was an acquaintance of his, about that jaunt. Tenney learned that the party had traveled to the Zuni Salt Lake vicinity where they spent several more days working that terrain. After that, Shaw went on to the northeast to the malpais flow.[3]

On one of his trips, Captain Shaw went into Fort Wingate and looked up the post trader. Although the fort had been moved closer to Gallup by that time, the same man who had supplied the provisions party for the original expedition was still in charge of the post stores.

He remembered when the men were there, buying food items, tools, and materials with which they could build sluice boxes. They had come in about noon and were in a big hurry to purchase the supplies and get back on the trail. They paid for the goods with coarse gold and told about finding the metal out in the malpais. Whether or not this last statement is true remains to be proven. At least up to now, 130 years after the fact, no large amount of gold has ever been found in that area.

Throughout the 1880s and 1890s, the story of the Lost Adams Mine spread across the frontier. While Adams and Captain Shaw were making efforts to find the canyon of gold, so were many others, one of whom was a man by the name of John Dowling.[4]

In 1881, Dowling was in Socorro, where he met a doctor by the name of Sturgeon. The doctor had need of a mining engineer, or someone who knew something about mining and about the western part of New Mexico. Dowling fit the bill in both cases. As it turned out, the good doctor had quite a story to tell.

In the fall of 1864, Sturgeon was with a party of cavalry scouts near the border of the territories of Arizona and New Mexico when two men, near death from exposure, limped into their camp. Sturgeon, having medical training, was given the responsibility of caring for them. One of the two pathetic lumps of humanity was named Adams. In the days that followed, the two regained their strength and the younger man (Adams) told his incredible tale for the first time. His listener was, of course, Dr. Sturgeon.

As well as telling him the story, Adams gave the doctor a map that was drawn in pencil on tablet paper, showing landmarks in the vicinity of the find. At the time, the whole thing seemed to Sturgeon to be just another casualty of the ongoing Indian wars. Later, however, when he had left the army and gone into practice in faraway Toledo, Ohio, thoughts about the Adams gold burned in his mind until finally, seventeen years later, he decided to do something about it.

The doctor organized a large group of businessmen, forty in number, to journey to New Mexico to find the well-known Lost Adams. By the time the "Forty Thieves," as they called themselves, reached Socorro, there was a great deal of friction in their ranks. The expedition fell apart before even reaching the search area. It was then that Dr. Sturgeon sought out and found John Dowling.

Dowling was already interested in the Adams story, and he was simply spellbound by the doctor's account. When Sturgeon produced the wrinkled, pencil-drawn map, Dowling's enthusiasm peaked. Something on the map stirred a memory from his past. He told the doctor that he thought he knew the settings of the landmarks.

Dr. Sturgeon was impressed and made an offer to outfit his new partner for the trip.

There was one thing, however, that the doctor insisted upon and that was inclusion in the party of one of Sturgeon's friends from Toledo. This friend was to go along as the doctor's representative. Right from the start, Dowling was against the idea, but the doctor held firm. Unless this man was included, there would be no expedition. Dowling finally agreed.

In the early spring of 1881, Dowling's small party left the village of Socorro and headed west. In addition to Dowling, the party included two men in their early twenties who worked for Dowling, and the dude from Toledo.

From the beginning, the dude would have no part in helping with everyday chores that have to be taken care of by all so that everyone could have some degree of comfort. Each night, that attitude nourished hostility in the two younger men when they had to do their own work and his.

Then, one afternoon, Dowling spotted what he thought was one of the landmarks shown on the penciled map. He saw two mountains that he believed were the two haystack peaks. If he was right, they were nearing the area with that unusual canyon—the one with the burned-out cabin. By now, however, tension had grown between his men and the dude, and he did not know how much longer he could keep the peace. Dowling was in a race for time and he knew it.

Now that they were so close, Dowling pushed on until late that day. When finally they stopped that night, the four did not bother with a camp fire. They just laid out their bedrolls and turned in, the dude going hungry and the tired younger men chewing jerky for nourishment.

The next morning, they rode into a long canyon and followed it for several miles to a fork. There, Dowling instructed his two employees to take the canyon that cut off to the right. He pointed to a high, rock-rimmed ridge visible several miles to the west and told them to meet him on that ridge as soon as they could work their way up there. Dowling planned to take the dude with him and accordingly, started up the left fork.

Before the two parties drifted apart, Dowling further instructed the younger men to keep their eyes open for a pile of rocks, natural on one side and burned black on the other. He told them that such a pile of charred stone could be the remains of the fireplace chimney of the burned-out cabin for which they were looking.

About an hour later, Dowling spotted something unusual. What he saw had never entered his mind before, but it (or they) tied in nicely with what he was looking for. Off to their left were *cut-off stumps* of what he guessed to be thirty to forty trees.

That's right, Dowling thought to himself. *There would be stumps from cutting the logs for the cabin.* He glanced at the dude, but the dude had not seen the stumps. Without knowing exactly why, Dowling decided not to say anything about the stumps, not just yet. He looked off to the left again, but could not see anything that looked like a pile of rocks. By then, he had managed to slip a little behind the dude. That way, he could look around and not be obvious as to what he was doing.

Suddenly he saw it. Off to the right and down closer to the floor of the ravine was a decaying pile of rubble—the ends of three or four burned logs and a pile of large rocks—some blackened. In his pocket was Sturgeon's map, but he did not want to take it out just then. Dowling thought about that map, though, and how it had shown a cabin near a running stream. If in August and September the seasonal rains had come, there would have been water in the ravine. A flowing spring would have had the same effect.

Dowling watched the other man carefully now, but the dude had been watching a playful squirrel and had missed the pile of rubble.

As they eased on up the canyon, which was now beginning to narrow, Dowling took notice of the physical qualities of the terrain around them. He planned to come back in the morning and check this out carefully.

In camp that night, there were words between the men once again. This time, the strained situation reached the point where guns were brandished. Dowling found himself in the unpopular position of having to defend the dude's life. He felt a responsibility to Dr. Sturgeon to protect his friend, but this was nearing the point beyond which he would have no control.

That made Dowling angry, and he announced to them all that at first light, they would be heading back to Socorro! Their gold hunt was over!

There was no sleep for Dowling that night; he was so close to what might be termed one of the greatest treasures on earth. However, if he tried to share what he had seen with the others, someone might die. The more he pondered the problem, the more he realized the gold (if it really was there) would only make matters worse.

Dowling turned back his bedroll and got up. He walked out on the ridge that had been their meeting place the evening before. It had been a beautiful night with a sky full of glistening stars and a three-quarter moon.

From the ridge, which was something of a high, narrow mesa, Dowling looked to the west. He saw a wide, descending valley with what he guessed to be prairie land beyond. In the east were the two peaks that seemed to be a part of the fading map. The entire scene held a strange fascination for Dowling. Standing there, he noticed the sharp bite of the early morning air. It always seemed coldest just before the sun broke over the horizon.

His eyes dropped down across the rough country that stretched out before him and he thought to himself, *This could be it—the Lost Adams!*

They rode along the ridge for some time before starting down. It was a long way back to Socorro. Dowling had thought it all out and decided that his main priority was to get the dude back safely. Then he would explain the situation to Dr. Sturgeon, and the two of them could go back together to investigate the canyon.

When they finally returned to Socorro without any untimely deaths, Dowling found Dr. Sturgeon was not there. He had been called back to Ohio and had left word for Dowling to get in touch with him when he returned. The dude left posthaste via the next train and Dowling was glad to see him go.

Without Sturgeon to talk to, Dowling's interest began to cool. He convinced himself that, after the dude had told his story, the doctor probably would not listen to Dowling anyway.

Only a few days later, another mining opportunity came along. It held the promise of certainty and a faster return than the Lost Adams gamble. Dowling did what he thought was best and went with the sure thing.

Nearly thirty years later, however, Dowling could not erase the old picture from his mind: a picture of stumps and a fallen pile of rubble. By then his age made it impossible for him to make the trip alone, so he decided to stake another man. He sent out another employee of his, with instructions and a map, to check out the site.

The man left and was gone about ten days. When he returned, he told Dowling that he had, in fact, found the canyon, the stumps, and the ruins of what had once been a cabin. There was, however, no gold in the old hearth, in the creek, the canyon walls, or anywhere else in that area. He had carefully checked it all.

About a year later, Dowling was told that the man never went searching for the cabin site at all. Instead, he had merely gone to the ranch of a friend where he stayed drunk until it was time to report back. By the time Dowling learned the truth, he was in poor health and eventually died with the unanswered question still on his mind. Was that the Adams cabin?

What may have been the same burned-out ruin was the object of two other searches. They were written about by James A. McKenna in his book, *Black Range Tales.*[5]

The first of these two endeavors took place in 1877, four years before Dowling's effort. Two men, Jason Baxter and John Adair, in a search for what was then known as the Schaeffer Diggings, did see the remains of just such a burned ruin in an isolated canyon west of Socorro.

Jack Schaeffer, another of the many Germans on the frontier, was cook for a detail of soldiers from Fort Cummings. In the fall of 1872, this detail was ordered out to protect a group of woodcutters who were gathering firewood for the fort near the headwaters of the Mimbres River. Bands of Apaches under Victorio and Chochise were known to frequent the general area, thereby providing the need for the troopers.

Though, he had never so much as fired at a deer, Schaeffer longed to go hunting. He brought this idea up to the sergeant in command, a man named McGurk, who told him it would be a good chance to get in some target practice. He was to go with another man by the name of Young.

The next morning, the two set out on their hunt. Schaeffer spotted a deer, fired, and the wounded animal fell down but did not stay down. It got up and ran into some timber with Schaeffer in hot pursuit.

Later, McGurk and Young located the downed deer, but their German cook was nowhere to be found. In trying to track down the wounded animal, Schaeffer had become totally lost and was wandering away from camp. A search was made up through the Black Range, across the San Agustin Plains, into and across a number of other ranges; all of the searching was to no avail. They did not find their German cook.

Sometime later, troops from Fort Craig came to Fort Cummings with word that after days of wandering, Schaeffer had made it into Fort Craig. His clothes were in rags, his boots worn through, and he was incoherent. He was still clutching his haversack which had once held his food rations but which now contained what the Fort Craig soldiers estimated to be ten pounds of gold nuggets.

After he had recovered enough to talk about his strange experience, he said that all he could remember was that he had seen a mountain on the side of which brush had created a picture of a women. He had crossed a wide desert or plain and had seen several herds of wild horses and antelope. Schaeffer did not know where he had been or where he had picked up the gold.

Jason Baxter heard this story from Sergeant McGurk in 1876. At the time, they were both stationed at Fort Thomas, located several miles northwest of the present Arizona town of Safford. Sergeant McGurk said that Schaeffer had enough food in the haversack to last at least two days and that after becoming lost he would not have parted with the food even for the gold. From this, Baxter estimated that Schaeffer had found the gold on the fourth or fifth day of his wandering. He thought the desert Schaeffer had crossed was the San Agustin Plains and that Schaeffer had seen what the early Spaniards had called Lady of Magdalena, a mountain-side where rock outcroppings and brush had, indeed, formed the illusion of a woman's face.

In telling this story to McKenna, Baxter compared Schaeffer's find with still another strike by a man named Snively. In the sixties, Snively came into Fort West, located on the Gila River near present day Cliff, New Mexico, with a collection of gold nuggets valued at about ten thousand dollars. At the time, Snively claimed that Indians had run him out of a gold-bearing gulch about 125 miles north of the fort.

Baxter was convinced that the Snively, the Schaeffer, and the Adams Diggings were all one and the same. Accordingly, after his enlistment was up, Baxter joined forces with John Adair and the two of them made their attempt at locating the gold of these three stories, all of which may well have come from the same place.

To add to their ardor on the subject, Adair had his own version. The following is a quote from McKenna's *Black Range Tales*.

> John had a tale of some rich diggin's which sheep herders told of, havin' seen nuggets in the hands of the Indians, the latter declarin' they had got the nuggets in a small gulch north and west of Socorro, a town on the Rio Grande.[6]

It was part of Snively's story that he believed sheep-herders had a knowledge of the gulch where he found his gold, because there had been signs of a previous camp. Would that have been Adams' camp?

McKenna's account of Jason Baxter and John Adair's try for the gold, told about their trip from Silver City northward. It took them up through what is now the Gila Wilderness Area, to the Elk and Tularosa Mountains, across the San Agustin Plains, and finally across the Datil Range.

In a setting of foothills and canyons, the two had made camp and gotten into a fight for their lives with Indians. John was wounded in the foot. Sometime after nightfall during a violent thunderstorm, the pair escaped from a pinned-down position and worked their way up a flooding canyon.

Courtesy Lt. Col. Ernie Allen, USAF Ret.
The San Agustin Plains (An Ancient Lake Bed) Where Today's "Very Large Array"—The Largest Radio Telescope in the World—Has been Constructed. The Vast, Flat Area of the Ancient Lake Bed Provided the Perfect Setting for the 27 Dishes of the "Very Large Array."

"John had to stop to put on his shoes, and neither of us could ever figure how he got the shoe over his swollen foot nor how he managed to walk after that, but he did both, whisperin' to me between thunderclaps, that we were between the devil and the deep sea and we would sure drown if we didn't get out of that gulch in a hurry. Hardly had he said this when the lightnin showed us the Mexican mule comin' towards us, still draggin' the lariat rope, probably havin' been driven down by the floodin' waters. He stopped and I caught hold of the rope. John made a halter of it and was soon astraddle. A little farther on we turned into a smaller canyon where the waters were neither so deep nor so swift. The sky became lighter as we went up this gulch which led us finally into quite a valley.

"By the lightnin' flashes we made out an old partly–burned log cabin standin' to one side of the valley. There was no roof and only a few logs were standin'. Close to the ruined cabin we also made out what looked like a sluice box and a pile of lumber; and a short distance away thought we saw two piles of bones. As the Indians . . . had discovered our escape, we dared not go over to examine the spot."[7]

This fascinating and frightening night occurred in 1877. Eight years later, in 1885, when Jason Baxter could no longer ignore his desire to see the burned-out cabin again, he formed a party with two other men and once more headed north from Silver City. With him in this endeavor was a man named Poland, and James McKenna, author of *Black Range Tales*. The canyon they finally made their way to looked as though it had been at the epicenter of a major earthquake.

Baxter could not relocate the old cabin site. It should be remembered, however, that when he first saw the cabin—eight years earlier—it was at night, in a violent storm, and he was running for his life.

It is a matter of historical record that no severe earthquakes have occurred in western New Mexico for many centuries. What is much more likely is that storms, such as the one Baxter experienced in 1877, had, over the course of eight years, changed the appearance of not only that canyon but much of the topography of the region. A burned-out cabin with only a few logs standing could have been reduced to a pile of rubble and charred rocks—or less.

This was the story of Baxter, Adair, Poland, and McKenna. Was the cabin they sought the Adams cabin?

At the same time the above-mentioned efforts were taking place, other men were engaged in similar undertakings throughout western New Mexico.

Jim Cooney was one of those who made an important gold discovery. This was the strike that led to the
development of the once-booming town of Mogollon.
Gold and silver mining that originated in the 1880s was
carried on there, right into the fourth decade of the
twentieth century. Jim Cooney, however, lived only long
enough to get the thing started; he was killed in April of
1880 by Victorio's Apaches.

Some of Cooney's friends blasted out a hole in a
large boulder and entombed his body there, where it
remains today. The boulder is about twenty feet in diam-
eter and is marked by a silver-bronze plaque.* It has
become something of a tourist attraction near the old
village of Alma, in Catron County. Lying at the edge of a
forest access road, the unusual tomb marks the locality
of several other early graves.

Jim Cooney's brother, Mike, was also interested in
mining. After selling his dead brother's mining claims,
he hit the prospecting trail. He had two objectives in
mind. The first was another find that was made by his
brother on Turkey Creek, a remote tributary of the Gila
River. His second objective was the Lost Adams.

Mike may have thought these two discoveries were
the same because it is known that he spent many years
prospecting the canyons and ridges of the Gila country.
After that, he branched out and extended his prospecting quest to cover a great deal of western New Mexico.
Finally, thirty-four years after the death of his brother,
Mike Cooney died while still on the trail of gold.

In the last three weeks of his life, he made daily
entries into an ongoing journal of his activities. The

---

* AUTHOR'S NOTE: At some point in time, since the passages concerning
 Jim Cooney were first written, a thief, or thieves—of the worst kind—
 have stolen the silver–bronze plaque. The thieves probably never gave
 any thought to the courageous pioneers who put it there—let alone the
 ones who slept within the unusual tomb. This sort of activity is a heinous
 stain against our modern generation. It is a trespass that can never be
 forgiven.

notes of the last few days described an old man at the mercy of the winter elements. Such was the story of Mike and Jim Cooney and of so many others like them. They died as they had lived, on the edge of adventure.

One of the best known searches for the gold of the Lost Adams that took place before the turn of the century was the Patterson expedition of 1888. According to most of the reporting sources, it involved a group of seventeen men under the direction of Captain Patterson, a rancher from the Horse Springs area.

Early newspaper accounts told about the party's passing through Gallup around the middle of that year, on their way up into the Navajo Reservation. Patterson was another avid believer in the Adams story and he had spent years in the quest. He believed that the old mine was to be found in one of the canyons in the Chuska Mountains on the reservation.

Captain Patterson held a commission as deputy sheriff, and used the authority of that commission to gain access to the reservation on the pretext of looking for stolen cattle. Later, another member of this expedition gave the newspapers of that day his account of the operation. This was George E. Christilaw, an old prospector. The following is a summary of his story.

> On September 8, 1888, our party left Socorro (where the group was organized) and made its way toward the Zuni Mountains and Gallup. In the Zuni Mountain Range, Ben Swift, now a cattle rancher but better known as a miner, joined our ranks and we pushed on to Gallup. Near that settlement, and just before entering the Indian reservation, nine of the party decided not to go on and turned back toward Socorro. The remaining men continued their journey to the northwest, coming eventually to the San Juan Basin. At that time, all but three gave up the effort and started the trip home. Captain Patterson, a man named Al Barker, and myself [George Christilaw] continued for a time, working the canyons leading into the San Juan. In the end, we made our way to Winslow, Arizona.

Near there, Patterson's horse gave out, and he went home by train. No gold or silver in anything like paying quantities was found. There were, however, many out-croppings of coal; some of them had veins six to eight feet thick. A good number of the springs we came to yielded not only water, but coal oil as well.[8]

This story was told by Mr. Christilaw in December 1888. As we now know, the San Juan Basin and adjacent areas have become one of the important coal-producing districts in the United States. Gold, however, has never been found there in paying quantities.

When I first read this account, I could not help but think about how there was a second story here. Before this party even entered the Navajo Reservation, over half of them dropped out and went home. A little later on, over half of the remaining number gave up the effort. In reality, of the seventeen men who began this endeavor, only three or four made a real try at finding the Lost Adams.

When Dr. Sturgeon's party of forty from Ohio made it to Socorro, only one of them actually pursued the undertaking any further. This is the human factor and it is always present. When statements are made to the effect that all of the Southwest has been covered by hard-as-nails prospectors, one should always remember the human factor.

Why did Captain Patterson think the Lost Adams might be found on the Navajo Reservation? Was he simply following Adams' lead because Adams had once taken his own search into northeastern Arizona? Perhaps an even better question is, why *did* Adams take his own search there? To me, this became one of the more puzzling aspects of the Adams story, to which I offer a possible explanation in the pages of the chapter titled "The Changing Arrows."

Throughout the last years of the nineteenth century and into the twentieth century, efforts continued by

Captain Shaw, Langford Johnston, Charles Allen and others. Then, in 1915, two other men joined the ranks of the searchers.

Ben W. Kemp, coauthor of the book *Cow Dust and Saddle Leather,* and a cousin of his by the name of John Damron went into the Zuni area. They searched a large triangular tract from the Point of the Malpais, west to Ojo Caliente, then north to a point near the village of Manuelito and back to the Point of Malpais. This triangle lies to the south of the Zuni Mountain Range and covers an enormous, rough area.

Their interest in the legend came as a result of a visit Adams had made in the early 1880s to the cabin home of Henry Cox, in what is currently known as Cox Canyon, near Reserve. Adams told his story to Cox and his family. That family included Josephine, a daughter, who later married Ben E. Kemp. They were the parents of Benny W. Kemp, the author mentioned above as being one of our searchers.

In this case, we can see the course of the story as it was handed down from mother to son. That story has only insignificant variations from the accounts of Allen and Byerts, both of which were published after the above mentioned search took place. It is also quite obvious that Josephine Cox Kemp must have had some degree of faith in what she told her son about Adams, a faith shared by her son.

According to the Kemp narrative, while conducting their search they saw what Benny Kemp and John Damron believed at the time to be several of the landmarks Adams had mentioned. Kemp said they found what they thought was the creek to which the Pima-Mexican had guided the mining party. This was not the first time, however, that searchers were certain of their ground. Of the things that Adams talked about, they found them all—except the gold.

Points about this version merit close study. For one thing, this account came directly from Adams. Captain Shaw, Allen, Byerts, none of the other usual sources had anything to do with this narration. The words that were spoken that night in the early 1880s, were impressive enough to weather the years and fire the interest of a young man over three decades later. This is just another example of how people believed the man and his story.

In the Kemp version, Adams is quoted as saying there were three mountain peaks resembling haystacks.[9] While this is not the only text mentioning three, most of the stories state that there were only two. Even though this appears to be a contradiction, it could be an important clue regarding the landmark. In telling his story, Adams was merely recalling scenes of that original trip. It is quite possible that on at least one occasion, he saw a triad of summits that sometime later, from a slightly different direction, appeared as only two.

In going over this version of the story, I was more than a little surprised at how closely aligned its basic facts are to the ones laid out in the Allen and Byerts texts. I was surprised, because in this case, the source of the information is totally different. Still another alignment can be found in the great effort made by Kemp and Damron in the ambitious search they made. This is even more evidence of that unqualified faith in the story that was displayed by so many in the past.

As stated before, the Kemp and Damron search took place in 1915. Many attempts have been made at finding the Lost Adams since then. The collapse of the stock market in 1929 sent more prospectors and what were called depression miners after the elusive diggings; still they remained hidden.

In 1934, Congress passed legislation making it illegal for citizens of the United States to own gold except in the natural state, or in coins of value to collectors. Although large mining companies were not immediately affected by the law, the fixing of the price at thirty-five dollars an ounce eventually made the mining and milling of gold impractical for even the big producers, as it had long since done for the small-time prospectors. For many years, the industry was virtually at a standstill.

In 1974, President Gerald Ford signed Public Law 93–373 sent to him by the Ninety-third Congress. This law repealed the 1934 legislation, making it legal once more for U.S. citizens to own, buy, or sell gold. That action prompted similar moves by governments of many nations throughout the world; as a result, the holding and trading of gold by virtually all people returned to what it had been prior to 1934.

The U.S. Department of Treasury adjusted the price of gold to that of the world markets, and it has since been set by those markets. Once more gold soared, its value reaching over $870 an ounce in January 1980. Of course, in the years since then it has fallen to less than half that amazing level.

During that forty-year span, from 1934 to 1974, gold, and the mining industry associated with it, suffered irrevocable damage. Even when its price found that unbelievably high mark, it could no longer muster the affections of man that it once had. Somewhere in the nightmares of depression and world conflict, our nation developed a commerce that no longer gave gold the front-runner position it had held throughout the previous century.

Still, the mystery of the Lost Adams continued to reach out to those who heard the story or read about it; once more, a part of the adventurous-minded segment of our society took up the search. Terry and I are a couple involved in this present-day search and our story is coming up in a little while. Now it is time to introduce another crew that is definitely on the rolls of the above mentioned adventurous segment.

Bob Gordon, Dave Greenberg, Bill Looney, and Larry Johnson had come to Reserve, New Mexico, on one of their prospecting trips. They were following up on a story that Bob had heard, about a map carved on the surface of a large flat rock.

The rock was near a lookout tower, on an isolated mountain summit, in rough country southwest of Reserve. Local legend has it that the carved map is Spanish in origin and that, if its markings and symbols could be deciphered, it would point the way to an old spanish mine near Black Bull Peak, also southwest of Reserve.

Bob, Bill, Dave, and Larry live in Texas, and the four of them have been on the trail of the Lost Adams for many years. They are working men, so their involvement is limited to a few weeks each year. That limitation, however, is more than made up for by their enthusiasm for the quest.

The first time I met these four Texans was late in August of 1981. Terry and I were spending a few days at a house we then owned near Reserve. I had been cutting a gemstone, called bytownite, that is found locally. Along with our own quest for gold, Terry and I had developed an interest in collecting and faceting gemstones; on some of our prospecting trips, we had picked up crystals of bytownite.

Dave Greenberg was also interested in gemstones, so we did a little trading. He had some plastic-encased gold nugget specimens that were appealing to us.

As stated earlier, Reserve is the county seat of Catron County in western New Mexico. Catron is an unusual county, indeed. Ninety miles long and nearly eighty miles wide, it is one of the largest counties in a state full of large counties. In its 7,000 square miles, there are only some 3,500 residents. So, it is only natural that not much happens that gets by the coffee drinkers in the local cafés.

It was from this impeccable source that we heard about the four from Texas, and from that same source they heard about us. Since all of us were interested in the Adams legend, it was only a matter of time until we got together.

Upon hearing that they were in the neighborhood, I decided to look them up, but they beat me to the task. When they came to our place, I was delighted. It did not take long to realize how well versed they were on the subject; in reality, they knew more about the Adams story than we did.

Bob Gordon had been on the old trail longer than the others, and his knowledge of the subject kept us talking late into the night. He had a valise full of printed materials and allowed me to photocopy what I wanted. After discussing the many aspects of the legend, Bob told us about the rock-carved map. He said he thought it might have something to do with the Adams story, but that there was no way to be sure.

He showed us photographs they had taken of the unusual boulder with the drawing etched across its surface. The idea of such a map carved on a block of stone and sitting on top of a high peak in that isolated region held a certain amount of mystery of its own.

In the days that followed, I asked a number of people who had lived in that area for many years if they knew anything about the rock with the map. Some were aware of it, but none of them could date it. It had simply been there for as long as anyone I talked to could remember.

While the Texans were at Reserve, they went into the upper reaches of Pueblo Creek and did some panning near Black Bull Peak. Bob told me later that it was one of the roughest areas they had ever encountered.

Another trip that had been rough on the team, because climbing was involved, had occurred a couple of years earlier. They took their search into the Ladron

Mountains where they found an especially steep and
rocky range with little vegetation across its slopes.
Early Spaniards called it Sierra Ladrones (Mountain of
Thieves).

Located some fifteen miles west of the Rio Grande,
between Albuquerque and Socorro, Ladron Peak
acquired its name by being a meeting place of wide-
ranging Navajo and Apache horse thieves. Its 9,100-foot
elevation made it a landmark throughout the pages of
New Mexico's history and it remains so today.

Bob's crew took a dirt road from Magdalena and
went north to what was once the location of the early
Spanish settlement of Riley. They then turned northeast
to the base of Ladron Peak. From there they followed a
faint trail through an ever-rising arroyo high into the
mountain. They dry panned several ravines but found
no color. This was on the mountain's northwest side
where they observed mostly sedimentary formations.

Bob told me that the mountain had two small peaks
at its summit, but it was their judgement that these
were not the haystacks of the Adams story. The physical
characteristics of the Ladrones simply did not match
those spoken of by Adams when he described the landmarks of the legend.

Just after the end of the Civil War, some indications
of gold were found in the Ladrones. Evidence of early
Spanish workings have also been discovered there.

On one of their last trips, Bob, Bill, and Dave
stopped by to let us know they would be camping on the
South Fork of Negrito Creek, between Reserve and
Snow Lake. During its course, there are about three
miles where the little mountain stream flows alongside
Forest Road 141. For many years, campers have used
the tranquil setting for their campsites.

The Texans invited us to join them for supper. Bob
said that Bill was planning on cooking up a Texas-style
slumgullion stew, and we surely did not want to miss

that. Terry and I appreciated the invitation and made plans to go.

It is about forty miles from our place to where they had set up their camp. I remember thinking about the fact that we were running late. The road was good, but at the same time, it was graveled and full of curves and takes a little longer than a person thinks it should.

In the midst of my thoughts about taking closer to an hour and a half rather than an hour to drive that forty miles, it occurred to me that Adams and Captain Shaw would have little sympathy for such concerns.

From the elevated roadway, Terry and I looked down along the creek and saw our Texas friends sitting around their camp fire, waving to us. I mentioned to Terry that I hoped they had waited for us as I was really looking forward to that stew.

It was not difficult at all to see why Bill was elected camp cook. That stew was really great. We were a little late, and something about the cool mountain air and the smell of a juniper log on a camp fire did not fail to sharpen our appetites.

In all fairness, I must give part of the credit for that delicious stew to Dave Greenberg. He told me, as I was bragging about the feed and polishing off my third bowlful, "You know, Terrill, I did peel the potatoes and slice the onions!"

That remark resulted in laughter from all of us.

After that unforgettable meal, we sat around their campfire swapping theories about the Lost Adams. It was one of those times when I felt as if I could almost reach out and touch the past. For a little while, our situation was not all that different from other campfire conversations when the topic for the evening was the story of Adams and his long-ago adventure.

Across the years, there must have been a thousand campfires, maybe more, where the lookers-on tried to unravel this magnificent riddle. A waste of time?

Perhaps for some, but not for the six of us. We had made our study of the old story and now we were hooked.

I thought about Adams, Shaw, Langford Johnston, and the others and wondered if they were out there, just beyond the reach of the firelight—listening and amused.

Bob and his crew had discovered a contact point, a zone where a good deal of metamorphic activity is evident in the structure and texture of rock formations and where ore bodies are sometimes accumulated. This contact zone was near the road, and they had found a little ore, gold and silver mixed, but it was not in what could be called paying quantities.

After discussing the contact point, Bob told us about a trip that he, Bill, and a couple of Bill's friends had taken to the Zuni Mountains several years ago. That outing had been everything but uneventful. The following is the story of that trip in as near as I can remember Bob's own words.

> Having never been in the Zuni Mountains before, we had no idea where to camp, so we just headed into the hills on the north side of Oso Ridge [a long ridge spanning most of the range]. After going several miles into the Zunis, our vehicle began to overheat, and we had to look for a place to set up camp. Well, we couldn't have found a better place if we had known the area. We stopped in a beautiful spot with several quakies [aspen] for shade.
>
> As it turned out, our truck was almost out of oil, and we only had one extra quart with us. This could have been serious because the nearest town was many miles away. While we were sitting in camp, and trying to decide what to do, from out of nowhere came a Navajo boy riding a motorcycle. We were politely informed that we had pitched camp on private property, and we would have to move to a place on forest land. We explained our problem with the truck. The young Navajo understood; as it was late in the day—that was Saturday—he would bring us some oil on Sunday.
>
> He did return the next day, in the afternoon, with a quart of oil; with him was the owner of the land we were

on. Once more we explained about the truck, also telling them we would move the camp as soon as we could. As it was getting along toward evening, we invited them both into camp for a drink and some supper. They accepted our hospitality.

The landowner asked us what we were doing in the Zunis, and I explained to him that we were looking for the Lost Adams mine. Although he had never searched for the mine himself, the subject was not new to him. We spent the rest of the evening, and half of the night, talking about the Lost Adams. He told us that over the years, there had been many people in the Zuni Range looking for this same thing; of the ones he had talked to, our party was better informed and possessed more knowledge on the subject than any of the others. Before they left that night, he told us we were welcome to leave our camp on his land for the rest of our stay in the Zuni Mountains.

Bob went on to tell about an old grizzly bear that paid a visit to their camp the following day. The large female bear had given them a thrill when it came close to their camp before seeing them.

Bob said the landowner had taken time to show them part of the Zuni Range. He took them to what he thought might be the Little Door.

It was a passage between rocks that led into an opening, but it did not lead into a canyon as Adams described. He also showed the Texans a little gold, saying he had found it there in the Zuni Range.

Continuing his story, Bob said that during their visit to the Zunis they had driven over to the El Morro National Monument. To the west, they saw a mountain whose top ridges resembled the upper profile of a camel. In the western part of the Zunis, they found a box canyon complete with a small stream and waterfall that would fit right into the Adams story, but there was no gold.

In winding up his story, Bob made an observation.

I personally don't believe the Adams mine is in the Zuni Range, but then, I know a number of places where it is not. I do believe it is out there somewhere, and someday, someone will find it. I look because I love the mystery connected with the legend. I like to go to the mountains with my friends; and I enjoy being close to nature.

After he finished, there was only the sound of rippling water as Negrito Creek made its way downstream over the rocks. I looked into the dying embers of the campfire and realized that someday this long lost treasure will be found. When it is, this enduring mystery will be a thing of the past; the quest for the Lost Adams will be over.

Bob told me once that he had given some thought to writing about his efforts at finding the old mine. I look forward to his book. It will be of interest to anyone who loves the challenge of adventure.

6

OUR SEARCH—A MODERN ADVENTURE

The first two words of this chapter's title, "Our Search," form an allusion—not only to Terry and myself—but also to the people who have shared our interest in this unique and fascinating undertaking. Over the years, the quest has placed us in contact with a wide variety of persons. Most of them have a kind of urgency in their voices when they speak of their convictions on parts of the Lost Adams story.

As a result of seeing this widespread interest, I gradually began to realize that the legend has an existing soul or spirit. A spirit that was born long ago in the minds of those twenty-three men when one of them told the rest about the incredible valley of gold.

The spirit grew and was nurtured as the company expanded its effort and the story began to take form. Day by day, it followed the members of that first adventure while they went to their fate. Like a finely textured orchid, the spirit opened and blossomed in the morning of their great discovery; then it drank of their spilled blood in the night of their massacre and death. It thrived on the words of Adams, Davidson, and Brewer and since then on the words of thousands until it seemed to cry out, "I am here! I hold wealth and greatness, I am the legend! Come, solve my mystery!"

The challenge is there, all right, but is only part of the spirit's call. There are times when, in its own subtle way, the spirit allows itself the pleasure of being seen by human eyes and heard by human ears. Evidence of this can be found in the simple beauty of mountain peaks bathed in the failing light of an evening sun. And it is always there in the fragile sound of a mountain stream as its waters cascade over the gravel of its floor, seeming to whisper, "The gold is here."

Looking back now, it is difficult to say at what time our activities concerning the legend became an actual search. This is due mostly to the fact that our search has involved many different aspects of its own. The interest started when Terry and I first moved to Grants, New Mexico, and heard those unusual stories about gold; stories about gold that, somehow, always included the name Old Fort Wingate.

The fort came into being in 1862. It was originally established near a great spring at what is now known as San Rafael, about three miles south of Grants. Later, in 1868, the garrison was moved to a point near Gallup where a government installation still bears the name Fort Wingate. The Adams legend was born while the fort was at the San Rafael location.

Just by taking a Sunday afternoon drive around the area in which Grants is situated, one will have to admit that anything is geologically possible. Within a matter of only thirty miles from this west-central New Mexico city, that drive will encounter several different geological conditions.

One of these, El Malpais, is one of the largest lava flows in the Western Hemisphere. Overburden, covering vast areas of a much older lava flow, has produced a des-

It is the Perfect Breeding Ground for Stories of Gold . . .

olate desert waste that goes on for miles. Mt. Taylor is also within the limits of such a drive, and across its 11,000-foot slopes are thousands of acres of pine and spruce timber.

Reaching out toward Gallup, there is a wide valley of red sandstone formations; in still another direction, walls hundreds of feet high of different colored sandstones form an endless array of cedar-covered mesas. It is the perfect breeding ground for stories of gold, and of all the tales, the one about the Lost Adams fits it best.

Terry and I had not lived at Grants long before we realized that the geology of the region was not its only claim to the unusual. Long before the Spanish conquistadors and the U.S. Army made their respective intrusions, the Indian factions were here in the widely diverse fashion discussed in Chapter 4.

Ever since the days of those first intrusions, this civilization has had a great deal of adjusting to do. While the geology remained much the same, the vastly different cultures did change to a degree as they learned the art of getting along with each other.

Grants was born and, as it grew, so grew the melting pot of New Mexico's many faces of humanity. The uranium boom of the early 1950s added still another wave of humanity; many members of that faction wondered about the Adams gold, and it was because of this interest that we were first told the story.

The thought of twenty-three men becoming involved in an endeavor of this kind in New Mexico of the 1860s held a definite fascination for me. The idea that one Indian tribe (possibly more) may have known the location of such a hoard of gold only added to the intrigue.

This was the beginning of our interest in the legend, and thus began the first aspect of what was to become our search. That interest developed into a quest for information, a thirst that could be temporarily slaked but never totally satisfied.

I remember reading that the story of the Adams strike was told thoroughly in Dobie's *Apache Gold and Yaqui Silver.* At my first opportunity, I went to the library, only to be told that their copies of the book were all checked out. I asked the girl behind the counter how many copies they had, and her answer came as a surprise.

"We have eight, I believe, at the present time. There were more, but a couple were not turned back in. A couple more are being reconditioned, and the rest are checked out."

I remember thinking to myself, *That many?*

Evidently, my thoughts were obvious in my expression, because she added, "It's one of our most popular books. In fact, we have a hard time keeping a copy of it on the shelf."

I have thought about that conversation many times since then. It was a genuine indication of the unusual interest in the more-than-a-century-old tradition. This particular interest in the story can be partly explained in the fact that Grants is near the historic site of Old Fort Wingate.

Today, nothing remains of the 1860s post except the windswept flat where it once stood at the foot of the Zuni Mountain's eastern slope. The great spring, El Gallo, that originally drew the fort to that location, is still quite evident.

It was not long, however, until I did manage to get a copy of the Dobie book and my introduction to the exciting story as the author saw it.

Over the next few years, Terry and I were employed by uranium producers near Grants. Because of this, we were in a good position to hear what other people in the area thought about the Lost Adams discovery. What we learned over the course of those years was both enlightening and interesting.

There were, of course, those who had never heard the story. There were also the skeptics and a few who had a recollection of having heard something about it. Then, there were those with that slight smile and sudden alertness at the mention of what was obviously one of their favorite subjects.

Some of them could talk for hours on the Lost Adams; of these, almost all had definite ideas about where to look for the lost placers. Many were convinced the gold canyon was out in the Malpais, others were just as sure it would eventually be found up in the Zuni Mountains. This opinionated response was something we ran into, time after time, as we visited with people in western New Mexico and eastern Arizona.

Residents of Silver City were sure the Adams canyon was in the mountains near there, while citizens of Glenwood, Reserve, and Springerville believed it was in their area. This was a result of those first endeavors by Adams and Shaw as the two of them traveled to the various points in those early days.

In the efforts made by these men, and later by Brewer, there must have been hundreds of conversations with the early pioneers about that canyon. Through those conversations, the spirit of the legend grew out of adolescence into a full-fledged mystery.

In the latter half of the 1970s, Terry and I purchased what we hoped would become our retirement home near the mountain village of Reserve. We bought our place from a gentleman by the name of Bob Christy. Over a period of time we became good friends. Bob was a man in his early seventies at that time, and it was interesting to hear him tell of his lifetime experiences.

He had been a heavy equipment operator on highway construction and had many tales to tell. One night, the conversation got around to the subject of gold; naturally, the story of the Lost Adams gained its usual dominance.

For many years, the subject had fascinated Bob just as it had us. It was something he could discuss all evening long, and his conversation held our interest. He was one of the few we talked to who had kept an open mind about where the original strike had been made.

You could tell by his talk that he had given the topic some careful consideration, and he would argue all night on a point that had been the object of such thought. There were several of these points on which we found ourselves in perfect agreement, a fact that I found surprising more than once.

One night, our conversation developed into a deep discussion about how much of the Southwest had been covered by men in the pursuit of finding the Lost Adams or, for that matter, any raw gold. I thought I would get a big argument out of Bob on this one; instead, he was of the same thinking as I.

It had long been my feeling that the early prospectors worked the live streams thoroughly. Owing to a much higher water table back then, there were a lot more live streams than will be found today. However, there have always been more canyons that are dry of springs and running water. Of these, it is logical that only a small percentage were prospected because most of the prospecting was done with a gold pan, and the panning operation was much more successful with the use of water.

For me, the result of this line of thinking is the conviction that now there are literally *thousands* of canyons remaining unchecked. Bob agreed, saying there could be little doubt about it.

In the last quarter of a century, the federal government has embarked upon a geological mapping program that is answering questions about the geological make-up of some of these unchecked places. Notwithstanding, gold is still being found in areas where these mapping surveys have been completed.

I once asked Bob a question that had been on my mind for years. It involved road construction. I asked him about the cuts that were made through mountains and hills in order to keep the highways as level as possible.

"Did anyone check for ore? Was anyone looking for gold?"

His answer, while bordering on the sarcastic, was philosophical at the same time. "No, Terrill, we were doing a job; we were working by the hour building road; no one had time to look for gold."

In a joking way I told Bob that he may have missed a good opportunity. I knew, of course, that he was right, but still I wondered, *How big would a nugget have to be to get their attention?*

In my mind, I pictured a rock that Terry and I had once seen in the Denver Museum of Natural History, the Gold Boulder of Summitville. That was some rock! It was approximately twenty-one inches long, fourteen inches wide, twelve inches thick and weighed 114 pounds. It was twenty percent pure gold, valued at more than a quarter of a million dollars.

For many years, it had lain within fifteen feet of a Colorado road that was used—as an access to a mine— by miners. It was finally spotted by a bulldozer operator.

So, even though it may take years, anything can happen.

Bob had given me a predictable answer and one that was, for the most part, accurate, as did the dozer operator who spotted the Gold Boulder of Summitville. In reality, maybe only one man among hundreds, or perhaps thousands, under similar circumstances will ever see rare minerals as a side result of occupations in which he makes his living.

Longer than men have been using bulldozers, they have been on horseback riding herd on cattle and sheep. The same rule applies. They are not out there in the hot sun or blowing wind looking for gold.

Bob said it well, "We were doing a job . . . no one had time to look for gold."

Many people make their living in the mountains and canyons of the Southwest, but few indeed have the time or the opportunity to watch out for rare metals.

As well as those who work in the mountains, there are those who play. Many come to hunt and fish. We often see people fishing, whipping a fly line out over a meandering stream. Some of them have a creel attached to their belt, but how many have a gold pan tied on somewhere? The hunters are the same. Whether it is by use of dogs or with a gun, the hunter is there to bag game. The hunt commands his attention, his interest, and his thoughts.

Of course, some people do have a better chance at finding gold. How much so is in direct proportion to their motives for being out in the wilds. The hearty backpacker who wants to get among the tall pines and bubbling streams has a slightly better chance because he might find himself in close proximity to the metal. He has the time and he will probably walk along a stream picking up pretty rocks from its sandy floor.

The odds of his being able to identify the average gold nugget lying on bedrock in that stream, however, are not great. Even at that, he still has a much better chance at finding gold than a cowboy hustling a scared calf out of some brushy ravine.

Then, there is the rock hound. He is convinced that the best stones can only be had by getting farther from the beaten path. He has a better chance because he is looking for rocks. He also has the time and he is an ambitious soul who will travel far and wide in his pursuit. He will come closer to finding gold than the average bulldozer operator because he will not just leave that curious-looking boulder lying there. No, in truth, the rock hound will probably pick up a thousand rocks. Some of those rocks will contain gold, but the average rock hound will never know it. His interest is in the beauty of the rocks themselves.

The geologist, both professional and amateur, will be the best bet at finding valuable minerals. Gold and silver are found more often by people in this category than all of the rest put together. Because of the previously mentioned federal mapping surveys, much of the United States has now been examined and analyzed by professionals in the service of government agencies.

Still, gold and silver have been found in unexpected and unlikely places. A promising deposit of gold was recently discovered within just a few miles of the city limits of Phoenix, Arizona.

Because of conversations that Terry and I had with Bob Christy and others regarding the foregoing subjects, we reached the conclusion that, of the people who go into primitive and isolated areas, few will find and identify gold. In truth, only a small fraction are motivated to try. As a result of our interest in the legend, Terry and I became part of that small fraction.

To say that there are thousands of unchecked canyons requires more than an understanding of people and their reasons for entering the realm of the wild. One must also have an equally good understanding of that realm.

It is difficult, if not impossible, to gain such knowledge while driving sixty or seventy miles per hour over the modern highways that Bob and his fellow workers built for us. Cuts and fills that we zoom over in seconds took Bob and others months to create while operating bulldozers and carry-alls at three miles per hour. Doing that, a person becomes aware of how vast the country is and how many hills and canyons exist.

While Terry and I never worked at road construction, we did learn a great deal about the country. Over the years, we took our recreation in the out-of-doors, for the most part in mountainous areas. Our experiences include getting to the top of most of the mountains in New Mexico with elevations in excess of 12,000 feet. We have spent a good deal of time and logged many miles while hiking, fishing, and hunting in New Mexico, Arizona, and Colorado.

However, it was only after we began our search for the Lost Adams that our understanding of this immense region became realistic. We found that one thing we cannot do is to see this magnificent country as the men in the Adams expedition had seen it. That is no longer possible. In fact, it is difficult now to even imagine how it was then.

In today's society when we decide to go somewhere, we get into our cars, go out to one of the various highways, and drive to our destination. We never look around at mountain peaks to be sure that we are on the right trail; we do not worry about water holes ahead. But take away the highways, the railroads, the towns, and the cattle ranches, and it suddenly becomes a very different world, a much larger realm. Understanding this is a major prerequisite for anyone interested in searching for gold.

Without this clear perception of the Southwest and an open mind that concedes the possibility that parts of the country may still contain unknown pockets of precious metal ores, many have failed to reach beyond the level of skepticism. When it comes to this subject, there are probably more skeptics in jet planes up above than in cars on our highways. Very likely, more doubters drive over those highways than ride horses into lonely canyons, but it will be the man on foot who will best judge the facts because he will have the best perspective of all.

The first of our field trips took place in the fall of 1977. The area we went into was in the Gila National Forest to the southeast of Reserve. This was early in the game for Terry and me and was prior to the time that we acquired most of the publications we now have. Our motives, at that time, were split between an interest in the Adams legend and wanting to see the Gila National Forest region. We had traveled extensively in New Mexico's mountain ranges, but the Gila was new to us.

Mile after mile, we drove the forest access roads looking for haystack peaks and deep canyons, and we found them. There were canyons and ridges lined up in an endless array. It did not take long to realize that the country was just too rough. It seemed to us that the ter-

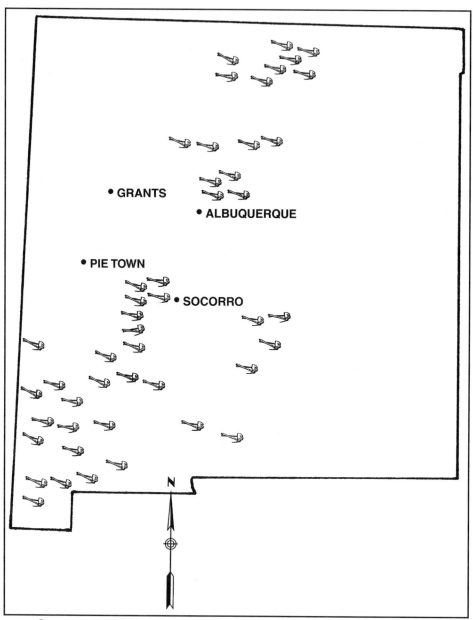

Occurrence of Gold in New Mexico With Pattern Gap North and West of Socorro.

rain was a long way from the malpais-studded prairies and juniper-covered mesas so common to the legend.

There are, of course, a great many mesas in the Gila region, but to some extent, they are something of an exception rather than the rule. More common to the area are the numerous peaks and canyons that form a rougher topography. Land swells tend to terminate into ridges rather than into flat-topped tablelands or mesas.

In the early days of the 1870s and 1880s, the Gila River country witnessed an influx of both stockmen and prospectors. This was the beginning of ranching and mining in western New Mexico. Gold and silver were discovered in many locations from the Pinos Altos Range, in the late 1860s, to mines near Magdalena that were first worked in 1881. Gold and silver were also mined in the southern end of the Black Range near Hillsboro and Kingston.

A major silver strike at Chloride Flat later gave Silver City its name, while only a few miles to the east, the Lake Valley discovery became one of the richest silver strikes in the world at that time. The strikes named here, and many others that were made in the closing decades of the nineteenth century, brought hundreds of miners and prospectors into the region now known as the Gila National Forest. Some of those people lived out their lives working the streams and canyons of this beautiful country.

There can be little doubt that, in the more than nine decades of the twentieth century, many others have made a similar effort. However, even though some gold has been found, no major discoveries have been recorded in the region during this century. Streams in the area will probably always yield a little color, but it is doubtful that extensive veins of gold, like the ones Adams searched for, will ever be found there.

Another problem continually plagues my attempts to locate the Adams canyon in the Gila Forest region. It is hard to comprehend why an expedition that originated in southern Arizona would work its way up into the White Mountains and the Springerville vicinity, only to change course and travel back that far south.

If the party went into the White Mountains and the area of Springerville, this pull back to the Reserve area is not logical. If the country around Reserve was near their destination, or on the way to it, more reasonable routes to that area would have been taken.

I know there are those who contend the Adams party was never in the White Mountains; to them, I can only say, research the story, dig out the facts! When you do, you will find that most of the early writers of the legend discuss landmarks reported by the survivors that virtually prove the expedition's passage through this range. These writers are in agreement on most of their facts.

One thing, though, continues to keep Reserve alive in the minds of those who search for the Adams gold. Adams came back to the little village, in those later years, when he sought to locate his elusive canyon.

Some of the old-timers quoted him as saying he remembered the San Francisco River at the point it now passes through Reserve. That could be, because at that location several small creeks come together with the river and form a colorful basin. The unusual beauty of that setting might well stick in a person's mind. Over the years it has become my thinking, however, that some of Adams' recollections were kept to himself and not discussed with those old-timers.

Throughout the 1970s and into the 1980s, Terry and I continued working at our jobs in the Grants area and as a result, our searching was limited to our days off. Even so, we managed to spend several days a month in the effort. When we bought our place just a few miles west of Reserve, it gave us a great base from which to work.

For over three years we made those weekend trips out into that fabulous Gila Forest around Reserve. At first we went south and east of Reserve, then we branched out and began checking to the north and northeast of the mountain settlement. Terry and I worked creek after creek in which we found some brightly colored agates, lots of mica, and once-in-a-while a piece of iron pyrite, but we discovered little gold.

As our collection of printed materials grew, it became increasingly evident that more consideration had been given to the region northeast of Springerville as a probable location of the lost canyon. This is where the problem developed in identifying the route of the mining party after they left the area that later became Springerville. The problem grew when Adams talked about those familiar landmarks around Reserve.

As if that was not enough, he led that one searching party into northeastern Arizona. Why? What happened at the Springerville location to so confuse both Adams *and* Brewer?

Trying to answer this question, among others, became more important to us than any further prospecting in the Gila.

As stated before, it was August 1981 when Bob Gordon and his crew came to our place at Reserve. At that time Bob allowed me to photocopy several articles he had in his possession. One of those was the Charles Allen account, *The Adams Diggings Story.*

From that time on, I have considered this version to be extremely close to the truth of the legend. Not long after we acquired the text, we moved our search to the Springerville area. We wanted to have a firsthand look at that country and, while doing so, check out statements that were made in several of the stories. A scenario we developed then seemed more closely aligned with the Allen Account than any of the others.

After spending a couple of weekends in Springerville, Terry and I decided, that since we were checking, we ought to start at the beginning.

It had been several years since our last visit to Phoenix; now that we had an excuse, we made plans for the trip. The point of origin of Adams' long trail, the Pima villages, is near Phoenix. In addition to this, there were a number of old newspaper accounts concerning the legend that I wanted to get, and I felt sure we would be able to get photocopies of them from the library archives in Phoenix. After several delays, we finally got underway.

It was mid-December when we made our jaunt to Arizona's capital city. That is definitely the time to go to Phoenix. While snow is flying over much of the rest of the United States, it is just right in Maricopa County. Temperatures there remain mild—much of the time in the seventies—the orange trees have a crop of oranges about ready to pick, and those magnificent palm trees add a feel of the tropics. It's funny how the beauty of these things escapes you when you are there in July and August.

We put in a long day at the libraries photocopying old newspaper stories about the Lost Adams. Getting the Arizona slant on the subject did prove interesting. Just as I suspected, however, some of the articles sought to locate the diggings there in Arizona.

After lodging that night in Mesa, we got up early the next morning and anxiously drove out Interstate 10 to Sacaton and the Pima villages.

In Sacaton itself, we found old buildings everywhere. Some of them had been there for centuries, and in most cases Indian families were still in residence. There were also modern structures and facilities which made Sacaton a curious blend of past and present.

On a side street, we noticed a long, two-story adobe building. It was deserted now and appeared to have been so for a long time. Midway along the old edifice, there was a doorway—minus the door—and a couple of window openings—minus the windows. A faded and decaying sign hung at an angle above the entrance. It read, CANTINA.

The dark openings were like magnets to Terry and me. We just had to have a look inside. Stepping from the pickup, Terry plucked a long-stemmed wildflower growing at the edge of the roadway. On an inside wall, there was a poster of a flamenco dancer. Her left hand was on her hip, her right hand stretched high over her head. Her whirling skirts displayed perfect legs and her eyes were nothing less than hypnotic in their stare.

Terry was standing in the doorway, looking at the poster, when a sudden gust of wind sent her skirt billowing a little above her knees. She put the wildflower stem between her teeth, placed her left hand on her hip, and arched her right hand above her head. Then, she turned and glanced at me with an impish grin across her face. I grinned back and warned,

"Don't quit your day job!"

"You're no fun," she responded while trying to laugh and frown at the same time. Then she added,

"Come over here and look at this room. Isn't it something! Can't you just see Brewer, the miners, and the Pima-Mexican setting around the table?"

"Yeah, and they're watching that flamenco dancer."

"No, they're playing cards! Seriously, they could have been here—right here."

After driving through the old streets, we headed out of Sacaton to a high point southeast of town. That is where we first noticed the string of settlements, eastward from Sacaton along the Gila River. While looking at them with binoculars, I relayed the scene to Terry.

"Well, now I know why the old writers nearly always referred to this as the Pima *villages* instead of the Pima *village*."

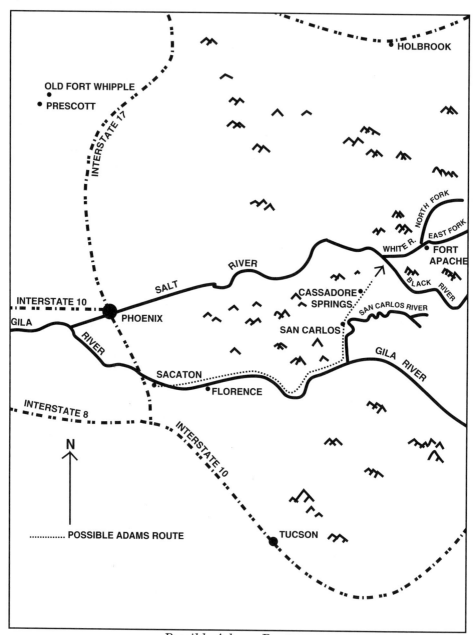

Possible Adams Route—
Region from Sacaton to the White Mountains

From what we had observed, we knew the Pima villages were a reality. They had existed for hundreds of years. Because of their status as a reliable supply point for the white race, at a time when many tribes were antagonized by whites, that part of the legend—its beginning—could well be true.

In the *Arizona Miner,* one of the old, early newspapers we found in Phoenix, there was an account by the publisher, Tisdale A. Hand, of a trip from which he had just returned. In the fall of 1864, he had gone to Tucson. On the way back to Prescott, where he published the newspaper, he stopped over and spent some time with a friend at Maricopa Wells, a settlement along the Gila River. During the visit, he and his host attended a fiesta at Sacaton. In reporting to his readers, Mr. Hand told of being favorably impressed by the Pimas and by their congeniality. He was also impressed with the many ruins of old villages along the Gila where the Pimas and their ancestors have, indeed, marked the ages.[1]

There are any number of ways to get to Springerville from Sacaton; to me, Charles Allen's version of the way the expedition proceeded seemed the most reasonable. Keeping in mind that it was August or September when this took place and the daytime temperatures were at their highest point of the year, both the men and their animals would need water accordingly. Water, therefore, had to be their top priority.

They were not disposed to bring wagons with which to haul water kegs, as well as other provisions. What supplies they had were carried on pack animals. This by itself would dictate a course near a reliable source of water. That course was to follow the Gila River as closely as possible to the place where the San Carlos River joined it from the north.

We checked the map and decided our next stop-off would be the town of San Carlos. It was located on the San Carlos River a few miles north of its confluence with the Gila, and that was on the old route that was described by Allen.

In the first one hundred miles upstream from Sacaton, the Gila River only gains about a thousand feet in elevation. That is just a one hundred-foot rise for every ten miles, and such would not affect the pack train. This condition did change as the route turned into the White Mountains.

We found the valley of the San Carlos to be a wide, dusty chasm between barren hills. Like the Gila, the San Carlos basin revealed no perceptible rise in elevation up to the small town of San Carlos. We stopped to fill up with gas.

While we enjoyed a can of pop, I asked the station attendant about the road to Cassadore Springs. He smiled. Then he told us the road was not the best, but he thought we would make it alright. I wondered about that smile, and we did not go far before I understood. He was right; the road was not the best.

For a while, we drove along close to the San Carlos River. Both of these rivers have water flow all year and would have supplied the expedition adequately. This route would also have kept the party on that northeast course. Upon leaving the San Carlos, the miners would have headed north and a little east for a matter of fourteen or fifteen miles to Cassadore Springs.

In that distance, they would begin to notice a little more upgrade because their trail would now gain about a hundred feet for every mile of forward movement. After leaving the springs, their route would take them into timber and across many mesas while working its way toward the Black River. Today, a gravel road winds through this maze of ridges and buttes to what is now known as the Black River Crossing. Then, it continues for a few more miles to a bridge over the White River.

Of course, it will never be known whether or not this road follows exactly the same route as their trail. It is a well known fact, however, that many roads and highways of today do follow routes that were once early trails. There is no question that a trail existed to connect the San Carlos River with the Black River and the White River. Such a transition would certainly include Cassadore Springs as a watering point along the way.

It was misting rain and a few snow flakes were falling as we crossed the White River bridge and headed north. The weather was changing for the worse so we decided to wait until another time to check out the White River part of this long-forgotten trail.

The Christmas holidays—and our jobs—put a damper on our hopes of picking up the trail on the White River for the time being. Then, January and February snows kept us by the fireplace and put a lot of wear and tear on our maps. Finally, March provided some moderate temperatures and that was all it took. We were off.

We drove first to Springerville, then on to McNary and down Arizona State Highway 73 to Whitewater, Old Fort Apache, and the East Fork of the White River. As our enthusiasm was renewed, our adventure continued.

In a number of articles, as well as in books, it has been stated that Adams and Davidson made their way to Fort Apache after the escape. If these events took place in 1864, as is suggested by almost all the accounts, the two men did not go to Fort Apache. The fort was simply not in existence in 1864. It was originally known as Camp Ord when it was first established in 1870. In less than a year, it was renamed Camp Thomas, then, Camp Apache; in April of 1879, it took the name of Fort Apache.

Right from the beginning, the soldiers and the Indians got along so well together that some forty of the White Mountain Apache braves were enlisted as scouts for the military. For the most part, the White Mountain people were an exception, rather than the rule, as many

Apache tribes fiercely resisted the white man's military establishment.

Old Fort Apache existed as a part of that military establishment until 1922 when it was turned over to the Department of the Interior. Eventually, it became a boarding school for the Apaches. Today, the weathering buildings provide an interesting landmark museum.

From the site of the old fort, we drove up Indian Service Road Y-55. It is a paved highway for twelve miles and travels right alongside the East Fork of the White River all the way. The average elevation rise during the course of this twelve miles is about one hundred feet per mile. Where the pavement ends, two graveled roads continue, one of these going north and the other south; both veer well away from the East Fork. It is about twenty-five miles farther up the river to the saddle near Mt. Thomas referred to in the Allen Account.

At the confluence of the Gila and the San Carlos Rivers, the Coolidge Dam backs up water for today's San Carlos Reservoir. From that point to the pavement's end on Indian Service Road Y-55, there are now a total of some ninety miles of paved or graveled roads. These roads could well be right on the trail the Adams mining party took if they did the logical thing and stayed near the rivers.

The White Mountain Apache Tribe has, at the time of this writing, a closure on a large part of the eastern side of the reservation. It includes much of the high country of Mt. Ord, Mt. Baldy, and the upper reaches of the East Fork of the White River. It does not include all of Mt. Thomas or the saddles between it and Mt. Baldy. At that point in time, we did not enter these areas. Instead, we acquired the U.S. Geological Survey topographical maps of that section and by close study, we concluded that the pack train could have followed the East Fork all the way to the Mt. Baldy and Mt. Thomas area.

The elevation changes become a little more demanding but, with the exception of the last mile that pulls right up to Mt. Baldy, those changes rarely exceed two hundred feet per mile. That last mile is quite steep, but even that situation could have been dealt with by taking a series of switchbacks up the mountain. In going this way, they would have had plenty of water, the protection of the timber, and a continuing supply of game for food.

There is another reason the miners would have taken this route, and it is just as important as the others. It was the easiest way, terrain-wise. Had they taken a course only a little farther west, it would have meant crossing the Salt River Canyon, the Grand Canyon's little brother of southern Arizona. Anyone who has ever traveled from Show Low to Globe, over U.S. Highway 60, knows well what I mean. We have the highway now, but back in the 1860s, it was a major obstacle and would have taken valuable time to cross.

Had they gone on up the Gila River, to the east of the San Carlos juncture, they would have traveled basically southeast, which would have resulted in getting away from the northeast course, on which point Adams was adamant.

The only other feasible route was to take the San Carlos River to its headwaters, cross over to the Black River, and then go northeast. The problem with this is the ever-winding course of the Black River. It would take much longer to traverse this route, which would eventually lead to the Alpine, Arizona area, with Springerville still many miles to the north. In reality, the course up the East Fork of the White River was, by far, the most practical way to go.

It was now mid-summer of 1982. As a result of our trips to Phoenix and Fort Apache, we had been able to see for ourselves the logical route of the mining expedition as it proceeded from Sacaton to those high saddles above the East Fork. This is the way they went, according to Charles Allen and we believe he was right. In addition to this, we were reasonably sure of the continuing trail out of the White Mountains and down through the valley of Nutrioso Creek. The question remained though, where did that trail go on to from Springerville? In this respect, we really had not gained much; but we had increased our interest in the story and acquired many more facts about it.

That same old, number-one question cropped up again. Where were the two peaks that Adams had talked so much about? That question, in turn, created others. What was he looking at and calling two peaks? Were there literally two isolated summits side by side? Or was it only one mountain with two or maybe three points?

Terry and I have been surprised more than once when a double peak we had spotted from one direction turned out to have three or more points when viewed from another direction. We learned a valuable lesson here when it came to seeing things in the mountains, namely, that it all depends upon the observer and his point of observation.

Perhaps the most obvious proof of this is found in climbing hills and peaks. There, every step up gives a new and subtly different view. Take ten steps up or down and the view changes considerably. Going around a mountainside or down into a canyon will produce the same result. This is one reason why people get lost quicker than they think they will. It is also one of the reasons why the landmarks described by Adams are not the easy things to find that we suppose they should be. Terry and I started two projects at the same time. We began taking soil samples in drainage areas and watching carefully for double peaks. When we spotted one of those lofty possibilities, it got checked out from several directions. Our ambitious plans called for working the creeks and canyons from Springerville eastward toward

Quemado, New Mexico. Access would be gained via the state, county, and Forest Service roads. Because of today's vehicles, and these many roads, we thought our chances of finding the old mine were better than the early searchers. After all, all they had were their horses and a few trails. A prospector, nevertheless, is still a prospector—and this country is still very big.

When we came to a creek we wanted to work, we parked our pickup, hiked upstream and began taking samples. Each sample, consisting of two to three pounds of sand or sandy soil, was taken from bedrock, when possible, and sacked up in plastic bags. Each bag was numbered and identified on a map that we drew up of the areas we prospected. Terry and I usually took twenty to twenty-five of these samples, anywhere from fifty feet to a hundred yards apart, depending on the terrain.

Later, in Grants or Reserve, we panned out the material. It was hard work at times, but it was also fun. We were able to see a lot of interesting country while getting some good exercise.

A few times we managed to get into what might be called a compromising situation. One morning, toward the end of July, we were working the country to the north of Luna, New Mexico and decided to cross over to New Mexico State Highway 32 north of Apache Creek. The two of us had never been that way, over Forest Road 216, and were looking forward to it. The sign identifying road 216 also bore the name "Centerfire Bog."

"What do they mean, Centerfire Bog?" Terry asked.

I told her not to be concerned. If it looked as if we were going to have problems with it, we would just turn around and come back. It was a warm, sunny July morning, and I thought to myself that it was hardly the time to think about problems. As is so often the case in that country, though, clouds can materialize quickly. We drove along for a matter of twenty to thirty minutes before the first sprinkles began hitting our windshield.

Suddenly, we found ourselves in a kind of broad swale with lots of deep grass. Our road had degenerated into two narrow canals through the deep grass and we had a slight problem. Then, to make things even more interesting, the sprinkle was increasing into a steady rain. Later, Terry described it as an unqualified cloudburst.

As we bounced along, I glanced over at Terry; she was sitting almost rigid, staring directly at the road, if one could call it a road. Her face was a combination of anger and terror.

Without ever changing that expression, she uttered,

"If we have a problem, we can just turn around and go back!"

As luck would have it, we had good momentum. Our pickup was half rolling and half hydroplaning across the wet swale. Apparently, our speed and the fact the old roadway had a firm base were the things that saw us through. About the time we gained higher ground, and put our "problem" behind us, the rain stopped and the sun came out.

We drove along a few more miles—without the hindrance of conversation. Then, I recalled the expression on her face the last time I looked her way, and I almost laughed. I asked her if she wanted to turn around and go back?

"That's not funny!" she said in a clearly agitated voice.

We never took Forest Road 216 again!

For the rest of the summer, we continued taking samples and watching for those two elusive peaks. When it looked like rain, and it did many times, Terry and I sought shelter beneath overhangs and wherever we could. On a couple of occasions, we found caves.

Mt. Ord, Mt. Baldy, and an Old, Old Clue

About the middle of September 1982, we were giving some thought to taking a hike up the West Fork of the Little Colorado River southwest of Springerville. Apache National Forest Trail 94 follows the West Fork up through the Mt. Baldy Wilderness Area to the summit of Mt. Baldy. In the White Mountains, the changing aspen leaves are at their prettiest during the first and second weeks of October, so our plans were formulated around that schedule.

The object of the trip was to continue checking parts of the Allen Account. The statements involved are included in the following quoted excerpts from that text. We take it up where the words are describing the miner's passage through the White Mountains.

> . . . up the East Fork of the White River to the saddle between Mt. Ord and Mt. Thomas, night camping on the saddle. The next morning the Mexican guide took Adams and several others of the party to the top of Mt. Ord and pointing to two peaks in a northeasterly direction said the gold was near those peaks. Adams thought one hundred miles to be the air line distance from Mt. Ord to the two peaks.
>
> Describing the journey from Mt. Ord to the diggings, Adams said the first day from Mt. Ord they traveled a downhill trail all morning and then came on to a mesa on which were two lakes about one-half mile apart, the trail being between them. That when full the north lake overflowed to the north and the south lake to the south; they night camped about ten miles easterly of the lakes on the bank of a little stream in a mountainous country covered with pine timber.[2]

Number one with us now was to see those two peaks, which according to the above were visible from the top of Mt. Ord. As a result of the Indian tribe's closure of the Mt. Ord area, we could not go to that mountain. However, we could, according to the Apache-Sitgreaves Forest map, take the trail up the West Fork of the Little Colorado River to Mt. Thomas and get close to the summit of Mt. Baldy.

Because Mt. Baldy is a little higher than Mt. Ord, we reasoned anything that could be seen from Mt. Ord could also be seen from the saddles between Mt. Thomas and Mt. Baldy; those saddles are part of the National Forest lands. They are also on the north side of Mt. Baldy and afford an excellent view of the country to the northeast of Springerville.

From where we parked our pickup in a parking lot at the beginning of Forest Trail 94, it is seven miles to the summit of Mt. Baldy. The elevation changes about 2,000 feet in that seven miles, but most of the time the trail is a gradual climb and not as difficult as one might imagine. From the beginning, the scenery is so spectacular we hardly thought about the upgrade of the trail.

The little West Fork Creek was a delightful thing to behold as it wound its way down from the high country. Much of the time, it came close to the trail supplying its share of those special visual effects. The trail itself takes hikers up through groves of fir, spruce, aspen, and pine. If a person is lucky, he might see deer or elk as both are prevalent in the area. Birds are everywhere; Terry had a magpie eating bread crumbs out of her hand.

We finally broke out of the timber and in less than ten minutes we were on a long-sweeping saddle that fell away from Mt. Baldy in the direction of Mt. Ord. The location of Mt. Ord came as something of a surprise to me. I should have known, from looking at the topographical maps, where Mt. Ord was in relation to Mt. Baldy, the East Fork of the White River, and other landmarks. Actually, I did have an idea, but when one suddenly arrives in the midst of these landmarks, what he had been looking at on a small map is displayed on such a grand scale that it is almost beyond recognition.

Mt. Ord was northwest of us, while Mt. Baldy was in just the opposite direction to the southeast. The East Fork of the White River was stretched out in a long valley to our southwest with its primary drainage channels coming right up under the saddle we were on.

I remember the question briefly crossing my mind: *Why would they go to Mt. Ord?* It was a good four miles straight across to that summit, and to get there would be no simple matter. There were several intervening ridges and valleys that would make the distance half again as far.

Six miles may not seem much, but when one has just pulled seven, as we had, one will have a clear picture of what only a few miles more can mean, especially when they are in the wrong direction. What this really meant did not have a chance to sink in right then. I was much more concerned about whether or not we could see what we were after from those northern slopes of Mt. Baldy.

Above us and off to the right was a sign denoting the boundary between the tribal land and the Mt. Baldy Wilderness. After resting for a few minutes, we started on the upgrade toward the sign. We had not gone far when the full grandeur of the White Mountains came into view. Like a gigantic hand, the East Fork seemed to hold the ranges in its grasp.

While I was taking in that mesmerizing view, Terry had walked ahead and was standing on a little crest above me. She was looking to the northeast and without turning exclaimed, "Terrill, look there!"

What I saw, even though I had fully expected to see it, was a scene that thrilled every fiber of my being. Off to our left and lying on a straight and level horizon were two peaks, cone-shaped and side by side. They looked to be about a hundred miles away.

Reaching into my pocket, I brought out a compass I had carried for just that moment. I turned back the alu-

Valley of the East Fork of the White River as Seen From Mt. Baldy.

minum cover and pressed the button that released the needle, then turned the body of the compass allowing the needle to accurately point to the north. The two peaks were *exactly* northeast of us.

It was a thrilling moment. I felt as though time had been suspended, and the spirit of the legend was now showing us what the Pima-Mexican had once pointed out to Adams, Davidson, and Brewer.

I looked at Terry, and she was beaming with excitement as she spoke, "You know what that is?"

"Yes! It's Veteado* Mountain north of Quemado!"

She nodded in agreement. From our high vista, Veteado had the appearance of being two, close but separate, points. We knew, however, by observing it from a

* Veteado–pronounced *Vet-ay-ow*

much closer range, that Veteado was only one mountain with two summits—a double peak. We were aware of this because our weekly trips between Grants and Reserve, for over three years then, had taken us right by Veteado Mountain more than a hundred times.

There had been occasions during those trips when it crossed my mind that Veteado might be the landmark Allen had written about. What made this hard to believe is that within twenty miles of Veteado there are several volcanic necks and peaks of similar elevations. So, how could it show up like this?

As I scanned the horizon, looking almost straight east, I could easily see the large timbered mass of Escudilla Mountain about twenty-five miles away. Only a few degrees to the left of it were the two humps of Mangus and Allegros Mountains in far–off New Mexico. Farther to the left of these rose the long ridge with the sharp northern drop-off of Escondido Peak just south of Quemado.

All of these mountain points were confined to an area covered by 15 degrees of the compass. From that point on for the next 120 degrees, or all the way around, past north to the northwest, the horizon was a flat and straight line interrupted only by the two points of Veteado Mountain.

Even though the view presented was clear, there was some pollution in the air and it occurred to me that 130 years ago, this same spectacular view would probably have been entirely free of pollution.

Looking now at the distant scene, we talked about the correlation between what we were looking at and the words in the Allen Account that had brought us there.

It was about one o'clock, and we had saved our lunch until we reached the summit. While we ate, Terry and I discussed the fact that the Allen Account was, for us, fast becoming something of a verification of the

Byerts text. This is true because Veteado Mountain is only twenty miles west and a little south of the *Point of the Malpais,* a major landmark in the Byerts article. Here were two writers, one of whom reportedly knew Adams, while the other (Allen) had worked closely with Captain Shaw; they had written this story down as it was told to them by these men. There are many facts about which they are in agreement. We had just found what might be considered another one.

We took a number of photographs of the area, including the saddle where we believe the mining partners had made camp; the valley of the East Fork of the White River; Mt. Ord, and Mt. Baldy. We also photographed those two distant points that we feared were too far for our camera to pick up. We took them anyway, hoping for the best. After one more look around, we started back down the mountain trail.

Terry and I kept watching Veteado as we descended. To our surprise, the landmark quickly faded from sight as a closer horizon developed. Even though we looked for Veteado, we never saw it again until we drove near to the New Mexico village of Quemado.

It had been the most fascinating day yet in our search. The two of us had stood at the midway point of that long trail that had originated in faraway Sacaton. As we walked along, Terry and I discussed what we had seen and how it seemed to back up Charles Allen's words.

I remember trying to recall the exact wording in the Allen Account as it pertained to Mt. Ord. I thought it had said the guide had taken the men to the top of that mountain to show them the two distant peaks, but I was unsure of the exact wording. As tired as I was when we got in that night, my first stop was the files and our copy of the Allen text.

I found, of course, that the Allen Account did indeed say that the guide had taken Adams and some of the

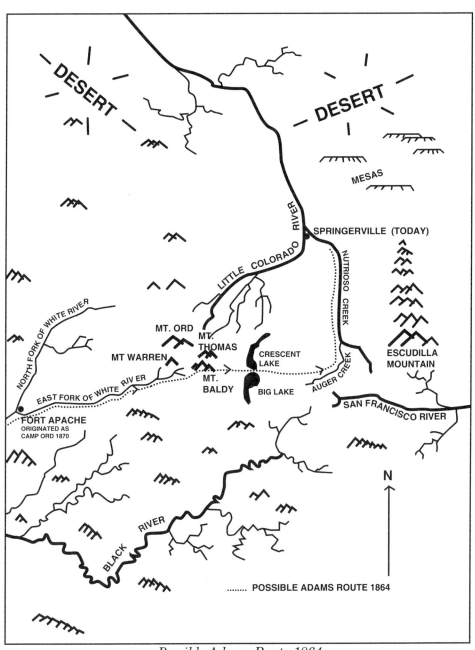

Possible Adams Route 1864

men to the top of Mt. Ord to show them the two-peaked landmark. Because of our trip, we knew that the high saddle spoken of as being between Mt. Ord and Mt. Thomas is, in reality, between Mt. Warren and Mt. Baldy. It is the high ridge to which the long column of riders would have ascended while making their way up and out of the valley of the East Fork. Mt. Ord and Mt. Thomas are several miles apart, Mt. Ord to the northwest of Mt. Warren and Mt. Thomas to the northeast of Mt. Baldy.

One possible explanation for what may have happened here is that Adams might not have been sure of the location of the various peaks, and as a result may simply have misidentified them. Or, I suppose there could have been a time when the mountain we now call Mt. Baldy might have been known as Mt. Ord. Allen was probably taking Captain Shaw's word on this, as it was told to him by Adams. If Allen had ever been to that high saddle, he would surely have written it up as it really is. This part of his text sounds much more like the story of the easily disoriented Adams.

Without a doubt, it was to the top of Mt. Baldy that the guide took his party. Its summit was to the east of their camp on the high saddle; thus, it was right on the way to Nutrioso Creek and the route that would take them north toward present day Springerville.

While we were driving back to Grants from that trip, I once more wondered why Veteado Mountain had stood out so predominantly on the horizon when hills quite near it did not. Seeing Veteado from the faraway White Mountains had given it something of a renewed importance. As we approached it, driving northeast from Quemado, it did look higher and more impressive.

Then, something I had almost forgotten came to mind. I asked Terry to hand me the New Mexico highway map we had in the glove compartment. One quick glance gave me the answer. Veteado, while not an espe-

Veteado Mountain, Lofty Sentinel of the Continental Divide.

cially high appearing mountain, was perched on some pretty high real estate to begin with—the Continental Divide. Most of the other hills in that area are not so situated, and those that are simply are not as high as Veteado. What we had seen from our vista in the White Mountains was the top four or five hundred feet of the two Veteado points.

We drove a little slower this time as we neared the double peak. At one point, the highway turns almost straight north, placing the mountain east of it. Then, after passing it, the highway turns sharply east with the mountain to the south. This gives excellent views of Veteado from two directions.

I have looked at this mountain many times; and have never thought it resembled haystacks. No, Veteado is not what Adams was referring to when he described two peaks resembling haystacks in the evening sun. At the same time, there was no doubt in my mind, or in Terry's, that Veteado *was* the landmark Adams had seen from the White Mountain lookout.

If we were right, it could mean only one thing. Two different landmarks were involved. Somewhere, not far from Veteado Mountain, there must be another pair of summits, which would probably look something like haystacks. We continued driving eastward toward the lava flow, but as I looked out the window at the changing terrain, I did not see anything resembling two-peak haystacks. It did occur to me my point of observation might be all wrong. The guide's words drifted back to me,

"The canyon of gold is *not far* from those peaks." I wondered, how far is—*not far?*

The twenty miles between Veteado Mountain and the *Point of the Malpais* is a treeless prairie for the most part. Once more, my thoughts went back across the years to that long column of riders. Did they come this way? Had we crossed that old trail? My memory dropped back further, to the Spaniards, the many different Indian factions, and the American frontiersmen. So many had moved through the area we were now going over.

There is a tradition that Coronado had camped at the *Point of the Malpais* and sent parties out over the lava flows looking for gold. Again it crept into my mind that perhaps the Pima-Mexican had brought the Adams mining expedition to the very gold Coronado had sought but never found. As we drove along, I wondered about this and about how great the discovery could be for those who eventually do find it.

As we drew nearer to Grants, Terry and I talked about making a trip to El Paso. We knew there were a number of articles published in the then *El Paso Herald* in the 1920s and 1930s; they might provide new facts

THE GHOST OF VETEADO

There is a mountain that's near here,
shrouded by a mystery queer,
for just half-way up its height there is a gruesome sight,
there is a grave.

Shelter such as nature gave,
and no soil conceals the bones
that lie there. Some matted hair
and a saddle lying near

Whether here some Indian chief,
brave, or warrior came to grief,
passed on to his hunting place, by his Mantaba's grace,
no one knows.

But when the air is quiescent,
and the evening is somnolent,
then the lonely herders tell, there's a spirit, seems to dwell
around the place

There a spirit seems to rise;
seems to take them by surprise.
Then they quickly cross themselves,
and slowly drift with their flocks.

He who hunts the errant cow,
up around the Veteado
when the eerie shadows fall, and a silence falls o'er all,
often hears a wierd call.

Now, it may be a cat,
but he takes no stock in that.
He spurs his horse, and leaves the cow
alone with the ghost of Veteado

Courtesy Carrie R. Emery

This poem, written in the 1920s by Martha Katherine Littrell Powell, bespeaks yet another legend rooted in this picturesque area. Vet-ay-ow is the historic pronunciation of the mountain's name.

and information. The important Byerts version was first published by the *Herald* and I felt that some of the other stories following it would be of interest to us.

When we did make the trip, we found that the Byerts text, because of public interest in the story after the first publication in 1916, was reprinted in 1919, 1924, and in part in 1927 and 1932. Several related stories were published in the twenties. Apparently, a good deal of interest in the Adams legend was generated at that time.

The publication of the different accounts brought forth people who were living in the El Paso area and who possessed parts of the old story that had originally come down from Adams, Shaw, Brewer, and those who knew them closely. Like the Byerts text, most of these articles advanced the idea that the Lost Adams placers were either in or near the malpais areas of western New Mexico.

During the depression, there was even more of a resurgence of interest, and many became prospectors on at least a part time basis. At one point in 1930, there was even a small settlement in western New Mexico called *Adams Diggings*. It was situated a few miles northeast of Quemado and boasted a post office until 1942. One thing it was never able to claim was that for which it was named.

It was now December 1982, and the snow had piled up on the ridges and saddles of the high country. The White Mountains of eastern Arizona were truly white, cloaked in Mother Nature's own mystery. Once more it was time to study the maps, and the new materials we had acquired in El Paso.

It has always been my feeling that in telling his story over and over to the people of the frontier, Adams imparted bits and pieces of information as his memory had allowed. Here is another place where the human factor must be considered. As the teller of the story,

Adams would have related the events as accurately as he could. There would have been times when his memory served him well and times when it did not. Details that he spoke of to one listener might have been forgotten in later conversations. It is also true that his listeners were capable of misinterpretation, or simply not hearing the story as he told it.

Of course the time factor is also there—130 years of it—and in that span of years, the stories and accounts have been published by the hundreds. In going through the copies of those accounts that we have, I seriously wondered, at one time, if there had not been two or three different men by the name of Adams who had been on adventures of gold.

An interesting point, but there was only one Adams and his story started with those bits and pieces. Even though that story has become diluted and fragmented, it is still out there. If one was wise enough to separate the truth from the staggering amount of fiction, the canyon of gold might still be found. Our attempt at separating fact from fiction became a monumental task in its own right and it is always there as a consideration in every phase of our endeavor.

Although the expansion of inaccurate fiction for more than a century was detrimental to our effort, there were compensating factors. Hindsight is better than foresight and we had the mistakes of all those who had gone before us to guide our decisions. For example, we now know the Malpais have been searched over and over without success. As far as is known, the area has not produced any large quantity of gold.

This same thing can be said of the Zuni Mountain Range which, like the Malpais, continues to be worked by a few hopeful souls. The Patterson expedition was not the first or last effort, by far, to try to locate the Lost Adams on the Navajo Reservation, once more without any known success. Now, because of hindsight, these

One of Many Old Ruins Along State Highway 117.

areas are a good deal less promising than they were once judged to be.

It has been rumored from time to time that gold, possibly from the Lost Adams site, has been found on the San Carlos Indian Reservation in eastern Arizona. If that is true, why haven't the Indians developed it? With gold going at nearly $400 an ounce, it is hard to imagine anyone or any group of individuals—including modern Indian tribes—knowing the location of such a discovery and not doing anything about it.

For Terry and me, the search for the old mine has been an interesting project, something different, a kind of hobby. It has given us an unusual insight into the history of a colorful part of the Old West. In that respect we have learned from this story of gold. Our learning process took us to many fascinating places like Sacaton, Old Fort Apache, and that high saddle on Mt. Baldy.

Quite probably, without this hobby, we would never have gone to those libraries in Phoenix, El Paso, Albuquerque, and even Denver. We would never have found those quiet, little valleys where wildlife has developed an existence probably better than that of human beings. Perhaps I sound sentimental, but our search has had its moments.

When spring came, we were determined to look for the two trails that had become so important to us in our understanding of the legend, i.e. the trail that led away from the Springerville area—and the *Wagon Road.*

In the collection of material we had acquired from Bob Gordon, there was an old 1864 map that covered the vast expanse of the New Mexico and Arizona Territories for that year. The major trails were indicated, but unfortunately little attention was given to local details. Our topographical maps were a little more rewarding on the subject of clues. On those maps, we discovered an unusual situation in the terrain to the north of Pie Town, New Mexico. Extending from near that village north toward the *Point of the Malpais* were quite a number of old ruin sites. On our trips to Reserve in previous years, Terry and I had noticed several weathered and decaying rock-house ruins alongside New Mexico State Highway 117 from the point it leaves Interstate Highway 40, just east of Grants, to the same Malpais Point.

Because of these ruins, two things became obvious. Water throughout this region had at one time been much easier to get than it is today. Secondly, if the people who were in residence in these long-abandoned structures ever got together, or traveled to whatever civilization existed then, there must have been a trail over which they journeyed.

That trail lay along a north-south axis, (just as Highway 117 does today) to the *Point of the Malpais* and then on to or near Pie Town. From the Malpais Point, Highway 117 takes a westerly course toward Veteado Mountain while a dirt and gravel road continues to the south toward Pie Town. It may well be that this current road follows the route of just such an old trail. In my mind, I wondered—*could this be the Wagon Road?*

It was about a week before Christmas when Terry handed me an envelope and announced,

"Here is your Christmas present."

I told her (in a frail attempt at humor) that I preferred larger gifts.

"Oh, you'll like this one," she said reassuringly.

It was a photocopy of still another Adams Diggings story.

"Where did you get this?"

"They have a rare book in the library called *Encounter with the Frontier* by Gary Tietjen.[3] Its about the early days in western New Mexico, and this chapter is his version of the Adams story."

In the account, Tietjen suggested that the two haystack peaks are D-Cross Mountain and Bell Butte in extreme north-eastern Catron County.

I picked up our copy of another book, *Guide to the New Mexico Mountains,*[4] and looked them up. It came as a pleasant surprise to find the two mountains situated north and east of Pie Town and a good distance to the east of the dirt and gravel road that Terry and I had thought might be the routing of the old wagon road.

At that time, our collection of topographical maps did not include those showing the vicinity of the two mountains. However, by looking at a simple highway map, it became clear that this was a vast region about which we knew nothing. It is isolated, partly mountainous and partly desert, with only a few large cattle ranches as its claim on civilization.

In the next two months, as we increased our knowledge of the area, it became evident that this isolated section could easily contain the remaining landmarks Adams had so desperately sought until his death.

In the conclusions that Terry and I had drawn from our experiences up to that time, we found a change in the way the arrows of evidence had always pointed. For many they have pointed to the Malpais and the Zuni Mountains as a probable sanctuary of the Lost Adams. Up to now, their pointing has yielded no fruit.

7

THE CHANGING ARROWS

Through the Christmas holidays and the first few months of 1983, many things happened that encouraged our interest in what was known as the wagon road that led to the old fort. The more we studied our maps, the more convinced we became that the present-day road between the *Point of the Malpais* and Pie Town could, in fact, follow closely the course of that long-forgotten route. We started calling it the *threshold* because of what we thought might be to the east of it.

One night we were invited to the home of some people Terry knew from her work. While we were there, our host brought out a large photocopy of a map that portrayed our state. Unrolled, it was three feet wide and three feet long and bore the label "Pioneer New Mexico." A note at the bottom gave the name Perry C. Van Arsdale, copyright 1969; it had been redrawn in 1983 by a man named Beecher.

Virtually every major historical event that had occurred in New Mexico was noted on the map, along with its location. The geographical positions of early

Indian tribes, old forts, Spanish and Mexican villages, and the pueblos were all shown.

After I had looked at the map for a while, it occurred to me to look for old trails, more specifically, one that could have been the wagon road. Then I spotted something right where we had thought the old road might be—a line of dashes coming north out of the country to the south of Pie Town. The line went through that village area and continued in a northerly course to the *Point of the Malpais*. Then it followed the routing of Highway 117 from the Malpais Point to the area near Grants. It was that portion of this line of dashes that connected the Pie Town area with the *Point of the Malpais* that Terry and I had thought could be the course of the wagon road.

Alongside the dashes was a label: "Ancient Apache War Route Against Navajos." In several places along the old war route, ruins were indicated. They were shown with the notation, "These Ruins Existed Before 1860s but Were Mapped in 1860s."

"How about that!"

Something else entered my thoughts. *Maybe, just maybe, the Pumpkin Patch was nothing more than an irrigated garden near one of these old ruins.* I made a mental note to give this idea more consideration later and continued to scan the big map.

In our investigation of those ruin sites, we were surprised to find that some of them were extremely old, perhaps as much as nine hundred years. Other sites were as recent as depression-era homesteading, while others dated back to Spanish Colonial times. The upshot of this is that people were there because of shallow water. Their connection with each other and the outside world was by means of a very old trail that was present in 1864.

Terry and I continued to examine the large map. It was a veritable wealth of information; a source that would take hours to read and understand. We agreed that we should have a copy and later found them for sale at one of the county offices.

This map is a rare example of how people take pride in their state. It took a long time to accumulate the information contained on this map because the history of New Mexico is so unusually full of interesting facts and events. The authors can be proud of their effort and in the New Mexico public that enjoyed it.

The wagon road, which we believe utilized part of the Ancient Apache War Route, could have been created by military wagons moving freight between Fort Craig and Fort Wingate. After leaving Fort Craig, such wagons would have taken a course similar to today's state roads 107 and 52. This route was in existence in 1864 as yet another trail.

On that trail, the wagons would have gone northwest to a point midway between what are now the villages of Magdalena and Datil. There, a westward turn would bring them along what has become the modern route of U.S. Highway 60. Here again, a trail did exist in 1864 and it led westerly to the location of today's Pie Town, crossing the Ancient Apache War Route there.

Turning north, the wagons would follow the old war route to and beyond the *Point of the Malpais*. Then, not far from present-day Grants, they would have crossed the well-documented Acoma-Zuni Ancient Way, discussed earlier in this text. After that, the military wagons would have skirted the northern end of the malpais, near where I-40 now exists, with a westward turn to Fort Wingate. This was the shortest and most logical route between the two installations. Considering the fact that Fort Craig was a supplier to many other forts, this theory is reasonable.

Terry and I began driving the part-gravel and part-dirt road from the *Point of the Malpais* to Pie Town during our weekly trips to Reserve. In taking this route we first became aware of the similarity between the massive Allegros Mountain, to the southwest of Pie Town, and Escudilla Mountain as it appears from north of Springerville.

At the time Terry and I talked about this similarity, something bugged me, but I could not pin it down. Then one night while I was going over the various accounts looking for something entirely different, I found the bug. In Ben Kemp's *Cow Dust and Saddle Leather,* a part of the narrative dealt with Adams and Davidson's escape.

> Their main concern then was to put as many miles between themselves and the Indians as they could before daylight overtook them. Adams said they traveled all night and came to an elevated plateau before daylight. They could see a high mountain far to the south, which they thought was Escudilla Mountain east of Round Valley [Springerville] . . . and they decided to try to make it back there.
>
> Since they were afraid to travel by day, they hid until dark. Traveling at night without food or water most of the time caused them to lose their sense of direction.[1]

If Adams and Davidson had made the mistake of thinking Allegros Mountain was Escudilla, it could explain many things. Such a mistake was not beyond the realm of possibility when one considers their state of mind, the fact that they were traveling mostly at night, and that they were doing so without the benefit of food and water much of the time.

In Gary Tietjen's book, *Encounter with the Frontier,* he states that years later when Adams was trying to return to his old strike, he could get as far as Horse Springs, New Mexico. After that point, however, "he was never sure of the ground."[2] Horse Springs is located about twenty-eight miles south of Pie Town, on State Highway 12. Allegros Mountain occupies an area midway between Horse Springs and Pie Town.

J. Frank Dobie and others wrote about Adams' returning to the Reserve area.[3] He thought he remem-

Escudilla Mountain Above . . . Allegros Mountain Below.

J. Frank Dobie and others wrote about Adams' returning to the Reserve area.[3] He thought he remembered some of the landmarks in that vicinity.

When a person puts this information together, an interesting question develops. Could it be that Adams was trying to get back to the gold by way of what had once been his escape route?

The following is our idea of what we believe happened to Adams and Davidson after the two of them escaped.

When the two survivors fled the scene of the double massacres, they did so under extreme circumstances. They would have been something more than human beings not to be running scared. To begin with, that fear made them travel at night; it kept them looking back over their shoulders, constantly watching for their enemies. Adams is quoted as saying that he and Davidson tried to stay near their incoming path. Under such conditions, it is certainly possible that they aligned themselves with the wrong trail.

Both their incoming track, from the Springerville (Round Valley) area camp and the old Apache war route that went through the Pie Town area would have taken them away from the massacre site. (This is assuming that the massacre site is in the country to the east of what we believe to be the wagon road.) In going either way, they would have traveled mainly in a southwest or southern direction, possibly mistaking Allegros for Escudilla Mountain in the process.

The wagon road was only a part of the Ancient Apache War Route. That route continued south from what is now Pie Town to the position of Horse Springs. There it intersected still another Indian track running east and west, one that by 1864 was being used by the cavalry as a scouting trail.

From the intersection, this trail led to the west, over the Continental Divide, and down into the basin of

Tularosa Creek, which, in turn, flowed southwest to its confluence with the San Francisco River. In the early 1870s, this juncture became the site of Milligan Plaza, later named Reserve.

After leaving the area now known as Pie Town, the Ancient Apache War Route went directly south to the intersection near Horse Springs; in doing so, it passed to the east of Allegros Mountain. If Adams did follow this old war route, thinking that he and Davidson were approaching Escudilla Mountain in Arizona, he would have remembered the original party as coming to Escudilla from the southwest; they had passed that mountain on its west and north sides. Now he and Davidson would have to do the same thing.

This could account for their losing the trail for a time, as is stated in some of the old stories, then later regaining what they thought was the same trail. If they did cross west of Allegros and proceeded south, the trail regained was the one that passed over the Continental Divide, down along Tularosa Creek, and on west to the San Francisco River.

We believe it is possible that, in their troubled state of mind, the two men could have mistaken the San Francisco River as a branch of the Little Colorado River, since forks of both of these streams flow down from the same northeastern part of the White Mountains.

After leaving the area now occupied by Reserve and by staying with the San Francisco River and going upstream, Adams and Davidson would have gone through what is locally called "The Box." This is a place where the river has, over time, made a cut through basaltic formations leaving walls hundreds of feet high. The resulting box is a landmark no one would easily forget.

Mountain ridges just north of this cut bear a visual similarity to the form of a woman lying on her back. In some of the old accounts, Adams talked about seeing a

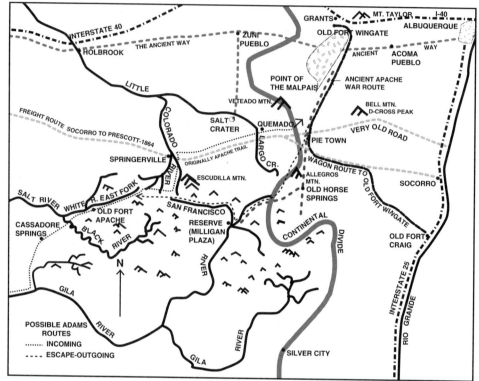

Possible Adams Routes

mountain, the profile of which resembled the outline of a women lying on her back. What is not clear is when, in relation to the occurrence of other events in the story, Adams saw this particular scene.

By continuing to follow the San Francisco River on to the west, Adams and Davidson would ultimately work their way back into the White Mountains and to the Mt. Baldy trail that had brought them in from the Pima villages in the beginning. The Allen Account tells us that the two men were found by Fort Whipple scouts near the White River site that later became known as Fort Apache.[4] That site, right on the East Fork, was also on the original trail. Here again, the fact that Allen had

Davidson's version of what happened adds credibility to statements like the one above.

There is no way to verify the idea we have offered here. It is only logical, however, that Adams and Davidson, in fleeing the area of the massacres, would have attempted to escape near or along the route they had come in on. If they had done this, their course would have been to the southwest. Whether or not they mistook Allegros Mountain for Escudilla, it could well be that the two found their way down into the valley of Tularosa Creek—a mistaken route, but wrong by only a few degrees of the compass.

In truth, there were few points of Anglo civilization at that time in western New Mexico. The only one near enough to be of any help to them was Fort Wingate. Nevertheless, the two survivors knew that, because of their escape, the Indians would be watching the trail to the fort. In addition to this, had Adams and Davidson made it into Fort Wingate and told their story, the gold strike would probably have been exploited right then and there. Moreover, reaching Fort Wingate would have given Adams his bearings; the orientation he seemed to be so completely without when he came back year after year trying to reclaim his lost bonanza.

In developing our theory about this escape route taking them down Tularosa Creek and west on the San Francisco River, it occurred to me that such a journey would have created confusing memories. For Adams to return after the passage of many years and to sort out the differences in those two trails (the one they originally came in on, and the escape route) would have been difficult for him to do, just as it would be for any man.

To Terry and me, this goes a long way toward explaining his indecisiveness in those later years. This confusion was obvious in his perplexing search pattern of region after region from Reserve, New Mexico, to northern Arizona.

On the big map, "Pioneer New Mexico," we believe that two additional early trails were involved in the story. The first of these left the Rio Grande at Socorro. It followed closely the route of today's U.S. Highway 60, a part of which we have described as being a portion of a possible Fort Craig to Fort Wingate wagon road.

After passing through the Pie Town area, it continued west through what is now Quemado to the location of present-day Springerville. From there it continued farther west, just as Highway 60 does now. On the large map, near the site of Pie Town, there is a reference to this trail: "Freight to Prescott 1864." Apparently, this route (one of those long-established trails the Apaches created for crossing Apacheria) was first used by freighters in the very year of the Adams discovery.

We believe this was the trail leading away from the Nutrioso Creek camp that was just two miles east of present-day Springerville. It took a course to the east-northeast from that Nutrioso Creek camp; in doing so, it crossed to the south of the Zuni Salt Lake and cart road referred to earlier in this text. We believe that the Adams mining party took this trail.

It is our further belief that their first night out from Nutrioso Creek was spent in dry camp on the high plateau between Springerville and Quemado. By the afternoon of the next day, they reached the valley of Largo Creek. There, giant cottonwood trees look down on sparkling water that does, in fact, flow to the northwest. In western New Mexico, streams that flow to the northwest are rare.

The second of these two trails is shown on the big map as "Very Old Road." It cuts away from the first trail, near the present-day site of Quemado, and proceeds to take a course to the east-northeast while the first trail follows a course to the east toward Pie Town. The second trail crossed what we believe is the wagon road near a spot called Tres Lagunas, a place where a small settlement once existed. From that intersection, this trail, "Very Old Road," continued to the east-northeast where it soon entered the valley of Alamocita Creek. It followed the drainage of Alamocita Creek to where the creek entered the Rio Salado River.

Along the Rio Salado, the trail went through the old Spanish town of Riley and eventually connected with the big trails on the Rio Grande. This was another one of those old Apache routes that came to be used by everyone from the Spanish colonials to those first pioneers who made the Pie Town and Quemado areas their home. Because of the development of U.S. Highway 60 and its forerunners, the trail up the Rio Salado River became a casualty of time, as did the covered wagons that once followed its course.

After crossing Largo Creek, we believe the miners took this old trail and followed it along one of the cedar-covered ridges that extend to the northeast toward Tres Lagunas. At that point they either crossed the wagon road, or as has been suggested, they may have turned onto the trail with the wagon tracks and followed it for a time before once more taking a course to the northeast.

The present-day road between Pie Town and the *Point of the Malpais* takes a course almost due north for a few miles after leaving Pie Town. After that, the routing is basically northeast for many miles before once more turning to the north. How closely this modern-day road might follow an early trail through this terrain is not known.

It is time now to introduce two more people who are interested in the Adams legend: Cliff and Inez Bixler of Denver, Colorado. Their involvement came as a result of the same fascination that the old story has held for Terry and me. Inez is my sister, and both she and her husband Cliff have always been high on the subject of adventure.

I had asked Inez to pick up a copy of a newspaper article about the Lost Adams that had appeared in their local paper. Then, when we were all together for a visit, we told them the story, and they became a part of our adventure. They took some vacation time during the spring of 1983, and we planned a trip into the country to the east of our "Threshold."

Because Terry and I were convinced that we had identified the wagon road, we were ready to look for more landmarks. There was the *Little Door* and others, but to us the most important remaining landmarks were (once again) the two haystack mountains. Naturally, they would be the most visible. In my own mind's eye, I had already found them and knew just what they looked like.

We decided it was time to investigate the two peaks Gary Tietjen referred to in his book. As stated earlier, these are D-Cross Mountain and Bell Butte. The two round-shaped summits exceed to a deceptive height as they rise out of the lower elevations between Alamocita Creek and the Rio Salado River. Their position is also near the northern union of Socorro and Catron counties.

In my thoughts, I had developed a growing curiosity about the two peaks. This came as a result of efforts I had made to spot them from Highway 117 during those weekly trips to Reserve. As that highway nears Veteado Mountain, it approaches the Continental Divide and elevations above 7,000 feet. From the time Highway 117 leaves the *Point of the Malpais,* it travels over a high prairie in a steady climb toward the divide, but nowhere along this route can one get even so much as a glimpse of D-Cross Mountain and Bell Butte. This seems strange since Veteado Mountain and the two peaks are only thirty-some miles apart.

After we started driving the wagon road route to Pie Town, I tried again to see the two summits from high places along that road, but without success.

It seemed to both Terry and me that winter and its disagreeable weather would never let up. When it finally did, Inez and Cliff made arrangements to fly in from Denver. Because her place of employment was near the U.S. Geological Survey offices in Denver, I asked Inez to bring us several topographical maps which covered the vast area to the east of the wagon road. They would also bring with them other maps they had acquired.

Before they were scheduled to arrive for that visit, Terry and I took a business trip to Albuquerque and made it coincide with our weekly jaunt to Reserve. This meant that we would be going directly to Reserve from Albuquerque. The route took us south out of Albuquerque to Socorro on Interstate Highway 25.

Then we turned west on Highway 60 and drove through Magdalena to Datil. Even though it was somewhat out of the way, we decided to continue west on Highway 60 at Datil to Quemado, rather than going the more direct route to Reserve on State Road 12. The purpose for doing this was to see if D-Cross Mountain and Bell Butte could be seen from the higher elevations along Highway 60. But the view that might have shown them to us was cut off, first by the Gallinas Mountains northwest of Magdalena, then by the Datil Range north of Datil, and finally by the Sawtooth Mountains northeast of Pie Town.

This gave us a new and interesting slant on an old question. These two peaks—that could not be seen from the west—could not be seen from the south either. With them, in their obscurity, was a region of several hundred square miles of a little-traveled part of New Mexico.

Our two Denver partners flew into Albuquerque, where they rented a car and drove to our place at Reserve. After carefully going over the collection of topographical maps, we decided the best way for us to see D-Cross Mountain and Bell Butte was to take Cibola Forest Road No. 6. This dirt road leaves Highway 60 about ten miles east of Pie Town and follows a winding course for another ten miles north to the Drag-A ranch house. The ranch house and cluster of buildings and corrals around it were once known as the McPhaul headquarters and were shown as such on some topographical maps.

Just before reaching the ranch house, Forest Road 6 turns east and eventually loops its way back to Highway 60 through what is now called Ox Springs Canyon. At the point where this forest road turns back to the east, a BLM (Bureau of Land Management) road continues. It passes in front of the Drag-A ranch house before turning east along the dry sandy basin of Alamocita Creek. For many miles, this road follows the routing of the previously discussed "Very Old Road." We put the maps away then and looked forward to our trip.

It was early morning when we left on the long anticipated visit to the region that seemed to be cut off from the rest of New Mexico. After a quick but delicious breakfast at Quemado, we drove east on Highway 60 through Pie Town to Forest Road 6.

In the first few miles from Highway 60, the forest road works its way through the rugged crags of the Sawtooth Mountains, an unusual range that, from a distance, resembles teeth of an inverted crosscut saw blade.

The sun was about an hour high when we drove through the Sawtooths and approached an intrusive dike just south of the Drag-A ranch house. From here we received our first look at D-Cross Mountain and Bell Butte. As I remember it now, I was both surprised and disappointed. Instead of two distinct summits that resembled haystacks, what we saw was a cluster of three points that were anything but distinct.

D-Cross had one clearly defined high peak; a second portion extended back to the northeast in a long ridge. Bell Butte formed the third member of the cluster. From where we were, to the west-southwest, that cluster did not look right at all. After we studied the scene for a few minutes, Cliff suggested that we drive on and get closer to the two mountains.

We took the BLM road and followed the valley of Alamocita Creek for several miles to the east, but the view from there continued to be three peaks. Driving on, the road split, and we took the left fork which soon turned more to the northeast. For a short time we lost sight of the three mountains. Suddenly, the road began to climb and after about half a mile we topped a small hill. From here we turned back once more toward the east. Our mountains came quickly into view from the perch on top of the hill, but now there were only *two*.

Inez verbalized it for all of us when she said, "Now that's more like what I expected to see."

I was elated, almost astonished, in fact, at what we were viewing. The scene was quite close to the picture I had developed in my mind. It had long been my conviction that in describing the two peaks he had seen as looking like haystacks, Adams was telling of an impression he had of two mountain peaks that really did look like haystacks in the evening sun. When it comes right down to it, there are not many twin or double peaks that will fit that description without a good deal of imagination. This was different.

What we were looking at was Bell Butte and the higher, rounded top of D-Cross Mountain just to the right and a little behind Bell Butte. The long northern ridge of D-Cross was concealed behind the bell-shaped peak. This was a prime example of a situation discussed in Chapter 6 regarding peaks with two or three summits. In this case, there were two entirely different mountains, one having two summits, the other only one. But clearly, from this point of observation, only two peaks were visible. We already knew, however, that from other perspectives three summits would be seen.

Bell Butte and D-Cross Mountain, Possibly the "Haystacks" of the Legend.

Just in the unlikely event that someone came along, we pulled over and parked beside the roadway. I wanted to take pictures of the two mountains. Then Terry made one of her profound statements.

"I wish the sun were setting."

With an affirmative nod in her direction, I thought, *How very much of a difference that could make.* Although I had always considered the sun's effect an important part of the illusion Adams had described, that part of his description now took an added meaning. I too wished the sun were setting.

The four of us talked over the possibilities of the two mountains being the old landmark; how they were barren, for the most part, with few trees; and how that would aid in producing the haystack effect. From our position, the possibility was certainly there. Even the shape of the two was not unlike large mounds of hay.

Driving back west along Alamocita Creek, I began to understand why I was never able to see the two mountains from the wagon road and beyond. A series of gradually rising ridges and juniper-covered mesas extended from the southwest to the northeast. I knew, by then, that it was between ten and fifteen miles across those high mesas to the wagon road. Somewhere in that country was a divide whose elevations were high enough to effectively cut this region off from areas to the west. To the south, stretching from east to west, were the long ranges of the Gallinas, the Datils, and the Sawtooth Mountains that Terry and I had observed a few days earlier from Highway 60.

After driving almost ten miles back to the Drag-A headquarters, it became apparent how vast this cut-off region really was.

Back at Reserve, we all took another look at the topographical maps Inez and Cliff had brought from Denver. The map showing D-Cross Mountain is entitled "D-Cross Mountain Quadrangle." Bell Butte, however, is shown on another map, "Pasture Canyon." These two maps together with one labeled, "Third Canyon Quadrangle," lie bordering one another in an east-to-west pattern. They detail the terrain from the Drag-A Ranch headquarters to and beyond D-Cross Mountain.

A second series of quadrangle maps named "Bonine Canyon." "Wild Horse Canyon," and "Wiley Mesa," when placed together with the first three maps, describe a block of land that is over 450 square miles in size of an all but forgotten part of New Mexico.

This block is the center, the heart, of the much larger 10,000-square-mile region discussed in Chapter 1 of this text. This heart section contains literally thousands of canyons, ridges, and mesas. Without any question, it is more than capable of containing and obscuring every landmark Adams spoke of as being near his strike.

It is our belief that this is one of the few places where the Adams gold could still be lying unclaimed. The simple truth is, few people go into this remote, out-of-the-way place, because without good roads the area is just another one of those ranching districts that has little or no appeal. No paved roads cross the 450 square miles, and only limited access can be gained over the BLM and county roads. These are fair in dry weather, but even summer showers can render vast sections of the region inaccessible except by four-wheel-drive vehicles. The only way to reach much of it is still by horse.

Our trip to see D-Cross Mountain and Bell Butte took place during the first week of May. With Inez and Cliff having only a few days, we spent most of the time driving what roads we could find that went into this isolated section. Terry and I realized that it was a good deal easier to talk about our theories than it was to get in a car and explain, in the course of a few hours and far more than a few miles, what had taken us years to understand.

The main point we tried to make to our new partners was the one that had become central and most important to us, namely, that had Adams, Shaw, or any of the early searchers been able to identify the two haystack mountains, they would have found their way to the gold. We also told them, because of our years of effort, that such an identification was no easy task. Adams, Davidson, or Brewer, having once seen the landmark would have had an advantage, but even then, they would still have needed to locate it again.

Our Denver partners had to return to their jobs and their lives in Colorado, but they left with renewed enthusiasm for the quest and much in the way of reading materials about the legend. They promised to return after the summer rains for another New Mexico adventure.

As stated before, a few large cattle operations run stock throughout this isolated and scenic district. Probably the biggest of these is the King Ranch. Its headquarters are about three miles south of the *Point of the Malpais*. Among the smaller ranches, there is a place that was, at that time, owned by Henry Lee Summers and his wife, Clyde.

The Summers land was located near the center of this remote block, and Henry Lee and Clyde are among the few whose lives have been lived out in this serene, beautiful setting. That is not only my impression of their ranch and its surroundings, but it is also their feeling after spending over half a century on the place.

Henry Lee was a young man, in his mid-twenties, when he first homesteaded a place a few miles north of where their ranch would later be. That was in 1933; except for a brief period of less than three years when they lived in Albuquerque and Silver City, the Summerses have lived the mostly hard, seldom easy, ranch life. Few people alive, if any at all, know as much about this remote and primitive region as do Henry Lee and Clyde Summers.

Our introduction to the Summers name came as a result of the examinations we had made of our topographical maps of that area. Their ranch is noted on one of the quadrangle layouts. Inez, Cliff, Terry, and I had picked out a place on our maps where we wanted to spend a few days prospecting for the Lost Adams. Since it is our policy not to enter private land without permission, we found the Summers Ranch location to be near our objective and planned a trip to the ranch to ask for that permission.

We were unaware of it then, but we were about to meet two fine people. They became not only a valuable asset to our effort but much valued friends as well.

During this period I organized my thoughts and began writing this book. It has long been a disappointment to me that some of the principal characters of the legend never wrote down their part in it. The old accounts that we relied on for the story are by people who knew Adams, Shaw, Brewer, and Johnston; the interest created by those writers has now evolved into the legend. How fascinating it would be, though, to read an account by any one of these four men. Of course, Terry and I do not fit into such prominence, and this text is not an attempt at such, but the story is certainly a great one and should not be lost because of the failure of modern adventurers to share their experiences.

Finding the canyon with its golden treasure locked beneath the hearth of that old fireplace will be the ultimate story. Ours is the tale of the ongoing search and the hope of writing about its exciting conclusion.

At that time, early summer 1983, State Highway 117—between Quemado and where it intersected Interstate Highway 40—was still not completely paved. There were some twenty-eight miles of gravel of which the *Point of the Malpais* was about centerway. By the maps, to reach the Summers Ranch, I took the Pie Town cutoff at the *Point of the Malpais* and went south for about twelve miles. At that location, I turned east on an intersecting road and drove another ten miles to the Summers ranch house.

The route goes right by the King Ranch headquarters; as I was not sure just how far that ranch extended into the area we wanted to reach, I stopped by to talk to their general manager. Most of these ranchers are fine people, but they want to be respected when it comes to their property and land, and I agree fully with them. Unfortunately, there are those who do not share that view, and they make it difficult for the rest of us.

At the King Ranch, I was told that the general manager, Mr. Bob Lee, had left a few minutes earlier. He was on a horse and should be riding near the road I was about to travel. Sure enough, about three miles up the road, I came across several riders, and among them was Mr. Lee. When he saw me stop, he dismounted and came over to the car. I explained to him I was wanting to get some information about the eastern border to the King Ranch.

I laid out my topographical maps on the hood of the car, and he pointed out the sections along their eastern side, also calling attention to other ranches in the area. I told him what our interest was in the region, stating that we would like to spend a few days there prospecting. He said he thought it would be all right, but that I should check with Mr. Summers because the particular spot we had in mind was on his place.

He also asked that we stop and see his foreman for those eastern sections so that he would be aware of our presence in the area. The gentleman was friendly and helpful and that made me feel better as I headed for the Summers Ranch.

Much of the land in New Mexico and other western states is still owned by either the state or federal governments. In some instances, the cattle ranchers own one section and lease an adjoining section in a checkerboard pattern. In other situations, like the national forest lands, great tracts of federal land are leased to cattlemen on yearly permits. The mineral rights, however, are retained by the government.

As I turned east off the Pie Town cutoff road, I could not help but think about the remoteness of these ranches. It was at least an hour, in today's terms, back to Grants; that was the nearest town. And the further back in time one goes, the more remote this area had been.

It was one of those rare, beautiful mornings; it was clear and warm. Rain had fallen during the night, and occasionally there were small puddles of water in the sandy roadway. For the most part, it had dried out nice-

Highway 117, Where Lava Flows Meet the Sandstone Bluffs—They Call It "The Narrows"...On the way to Summers Ranch ...

ly. This was my first trip into this particular area and I remember wishing that Terry could have come with me. Unfortunately, she had been called back to work. We knew, of course, that unless I got completely shot down, there would be other chances for her to see this picturesque country. It seemed to me that the farther I drove, the prettier it became. It reminded me of landscapes I had seen in some of the better western movies.

The elevation at the ranch house is 7,800 feet. As I looked around, it became apparent that someone, or several someones, had worked hard in creating the ranch headquarters. While my eyes scanned the surroundings, I got my first look at my host—and he had his first look at me. Mr. Summers was standing near a closed gate that led into a corral, about a hundred feet away.

The expression on his face seemed to say, "Who the hell is that? And what the hell does he want?" I will always believe that was exactly what he was thinking.

To say he was a big man wouldn't do at all. To me, he looked like a professional wrestler, especially from the waist up. His black, ten-gallon hat was the perfect crown for the rugged, westerner beneath.

I just stood there for a minute, trying to figure out what I was going to say to him. His dog, Connie, had enough friendliness for both of them; she kept expressing her friendship by jumping up on me until I accidentally stepped on her back paw. The action sent Connie away howling and caused me to lose my balance. I dropped part way to the ground, thinking to myself, *Boy, what a start!*

When I regained my composure, I walked toward Summers as he was walking to meet me. We shook hands while introducing ourselves. I told him I was a prospector, and I was interested in an area on his ranch.

He asked me if I liked coffee, and I assured him that I did. Then, we went into their house where Mrs. Summers was already setting out the cups. The three of us sat around their kitchen table that morning and got acquainted while drinking several cups of her good coffee. We discussed many things among which were politics, local history, and hunting, and we got along quite well.

Mrs. Summers was so very different from her husband as far as appearances go. She was small in stature but long on heart. She had a kind, loving, face that revealed both strength and compassion. That was my first impression of her, and over the years I came to know just how right I was in that appraisal. She is one of the finest people I have ever known.

It did not take long to see that the two of them were of the old school; their values were the tried and proven values that guide the wholesome and worthwhile members of our modern society.

I told them that I represented not only my wife and myself but also my sister and her husband, and that we would like to spend a few days at *Onion Springs* looking for gold. He nodded his head and said it would be okay.

Mr. Summers identified his land on the topographical map of that area and we talked about such things as the road into the location and the terrain we would find there. He told me others had been in the area from time to time, looking for coal and uranium deposits. In later conversations, Summers said that back in the thirties there had been a few "depression miners" going through the country looking for gold, but most of them, he added, never ventured far from their cars.

That was the way it went the first day. I felt exhilarated as I drove away from the Summers Ranch. They had shown me the kind of hospitality that has become so rare I was not sure it still existed anymore.

After driving a few miles, I stopped and wrote down my impressions. I knew then that Mr. and Mrs. Summers would become part of the story I was beginning to write.

The summer rains, occurring almost every day, are the result of moist air brought into the Southwest by monsoon winds. Normally, the monsoons begin about the middle of July. In 1983, however, the rains started during the first week of July, which prompted us to think they might be over early. Unfortunately it did not work out that way.

The last week of August came and went, followed by the first two weeks of September and still it continued to rain. Usually, these are not steady, widespread rains, but rather showers that would form anywhere at anytime. Once in a while, an area can get pounded by heavy downpours; when this happens, roadways are washed out and bridges are lost. Knowing this, we decided to wait until the rains stopped before entering the isolated area of *Onion Springs*.

Throughout the rest of September, though, it kept coming down. Then, finally, the sky cleared for several days; the weathermen on television said they thought it was over. It was time to go and look for a legend.

Our Denver partners were also ready. They came down and brought their van and camp trailer with them. The four of us were all set to spend our time looking for the Lost Adams in relative comfort.

We took along a special piece of equipment to help us in our search, something that Adams, Shaw, and Johnston did not have—the latest model Whites metal detector. Gold nuggets are sometimes found with metal detectors, and we thought it might give us an edge. We also had plenty of plastic bags for taking the all-important samples. We had water, food, propane lanterns, and battery-powered fluorescent lights. The only thing we were short on was time, but as we readied our equipment and prepared for the trip, time was the last thing on our minds.

We were all in good spirits as we drove over the sandy roads toward the Summers Ranch. By then, Terry and I had been to the ranch several times, but Inez and Cliff had never met the Summerses. I was looking forward to doing the introductions. As we entered their yard, their little public relations K-9, Connie, bounced around letting us know how glad she was to see us.

A short while later, as we were all sitting around their table, Mr. Summers told us about his try for gold.

Oh, it was many years ago now; I reckon it was back in the late thirties or early forties. I found a great pine tree, you know, a big one, exceptional size! And someone, sometime long before, had cut a blaze on the trunk of that tree—must have been two feet wide and five feet long. Well, I just knew it was some kind of old marker.

There might be gold down there! In fact, there was no doubt about it—something was buried below the base of that tree. All I had to do was dig it up!

I was a lot younger then, and I didn't think a thing about digging a little ol' hole. That first day the digging was in sand, and it was not bad going at all. But then I struck clay, and not long after that I was digging in caliche.

"Have you ever dug through caliche?" he asked, looking at Cliff and me.

Being from Texas, we both assured him that we had.

Well, the deeper I went, the more the hole had to be widened at the top. When I got through prospectin', that hole was ten feet wide across the top and eighteen feet deep. But, there was no gold, no treasure, no nothing!

When I got home that night, Clyde fixed me a great big bowl of chili. After supper, I sat down and drew up this picture of myself standing at the edge of that hole and it half full of my blood, sweat, and tears. Of course, I knew it was old Satan himself that put me up to it, so I drew him into my picture.

After Mr. Summers finished with his story, he passed the drawing around, and we all had a good laugh at his expense.

"I guess about the maddest I ever got at one of my girls was while I was digging that hole," he continued. "She had come down to help me—but she had forgotten to bring along a sack to put the gold in."

When he made this last remark, I choked on my coffee. He never told me which daughter he was talking about; he and Mrs. Summers raised five girls at the remote ranch. They had no sons.

"That was the first time—and the last—I ever hunted for gold here. Any time I'm tempted, I just get my drawing. Then, after looking at it for a few minutes, my lust for gold just drifts away."

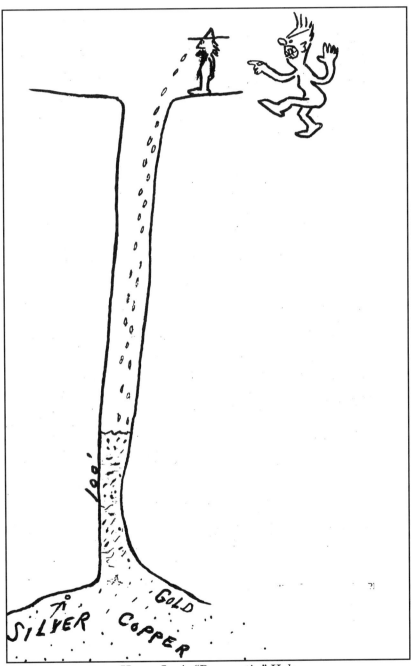

Henry Lee's "Prospectin" Hole

Once more, our laughter filled the room. Mr. Summers was smiling, but it seemed to me there was just a hint of seriousness in his eyes.

Before we left, he told us a little about *Onion Springs* itself. He said that it had been there for as long as anyone they knew could remember. When he and Mrs. Summers first came into that area, the spring had produced more water than it currently did. Wild onions had once been plentiful at the location, hence the name.

Then Mr. Summers recalled something that really stirred our interest. Several years ago, he had seen what he thought might have been two aged smelters up on top of *Tachado* (Tä-shä-dö) *Mesa*. That was a high plateau just north of where we planned to camp. Some of the canyons we wanted to check out terminated into the southern walls of *Tachado Mesa*.

The four of us were full of anticipation as we drove away from the ranch house and headed for the canyon area containing *Onion Springs*. I kept remembering those stories about how the early Indian tribes had filled in the mines, but had on occasion left the old smelters of the early Spanish mining operations. I had never discussed this subject with Mr. Summers, and now he was telling us about aged smelters.

We went by to check with the King Ranch foreman, as the ranch manager had requested, but found no one at home. After waiting about an hour for him, we proceeded on to where a seldom-traveled road forked off the county road we had been following.

Turning south, we dropped down into the head of Wild Horse Canyon. In the course of a little over two miles, we descended about five hundred feet into the canyon. We camped near one of Mr. Summers' windmills among several piñon pine and juniper trees.

Setting up camp was a pleasure. With the camper, we had all the necessities, plus the advantages of comfort. We did not, however, have telephones or television,

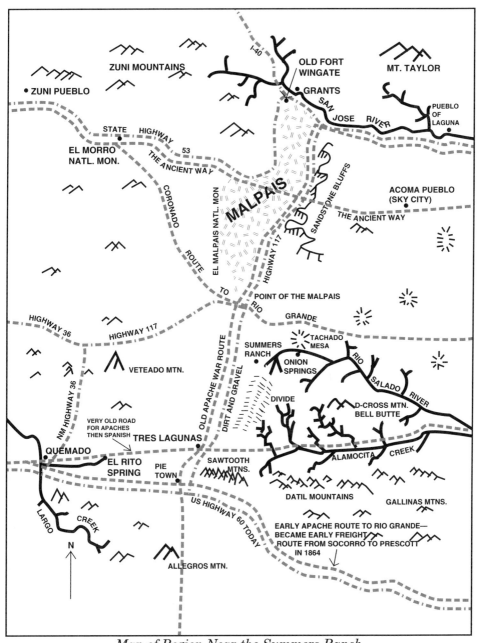

Map of Region Near the Summers Ranch

but these were not missed. Terry did find a radio, and we had several Albuquerque stations to listen to.

After the sun went down, it cooled off in a hurry. Then, just as it became dark, a nearly full moon rose over an eastern ridge. The moonlight gave the rough terrain around us a strange appeal. The combination of shadows and moon glow on the trees and rocks seemed to beckon.

"You know, it really makes you wonder about Brewer. How do you suppose he managed to cross all of these canyons and get down to the Rio Grande?" Cliff asked.

"I don't know," I said. "It's hard for me to believe he could have been much farther west than this and still have made it."

"How far is it to the river?" asked Inez.

"I would guess it to be about fifty miles straight across. To get there on foot, it would probably be closer to seventy or eighty miles. Of course, now there aren't any cantankerous people out there—or mountain lions or bears. At least, I don't think there are."

At that, Terry quickly looked up and soberly advised, "One more remark like that, and you might get to walk there, too!"

Overhead, the strobe lights of a jet airliner moved through a fabulous array of stars in the cool autumn night. For atmosphere, our radio was giving off the sound of a rock tune. The girls were fixing supper on the camper's propane stove. Cliff was taking a look at our metal detector; and I was adding another log to the camp fire.

I could not help thinking how completely different our world was from the world of Adams, Davidson, and Brewer. When they were here, in 1864, they could never have imagined such things as rock music, metal detectors, or jets flying through the night.

I thought about tomorrow and wondered if we would find what we were looking for; imaging how great it would be to see the place where those legendary events occurred. Then, I thought about the hearth of that old fireplace—and all that gold.

We were up at 5:00 A.M. and by 6:00, had left camp heading in a southeasterly direction following Wild Horse Canyon. After about thirty minutes, our walking brought us to the small pool of crystal clear water known as *Onion Springs*. For several yards around the pool itself, the ground was spongy and the grass deep and lush from the seeping water. We looked around for wild onions, but saw none. Perhaps the thick grass had squeezed them out.

I ran the metal detector over the area around the spring but heard only one beep. That was from a rusty can left by someone in the past.

After another half-hour walk, we found that Wild Horse Canyon merged with a slightly larger valley, and the two of them formed the beginning of the Rio Salado River. We continued a southeasterly course along the dry, sandy floor of the valley and soon gained sight of D-Cross Mountain and Bell Butte.

Here again, the angle of observation was wrong. This time the two mountains were to the southeast of us, and their appearance was even more of a cluster of ridges and points.

It was about 8:00 A.M. when we entered the mouth of a narrow canyon, our objective for the day. Before us was the long, narrow, winding gulch called Squirrel Canyon on the topographical maps. Extending more than three miles, south to north, it followed a weaving and twisting course to where it headed against the rising perimeter of *Tachado*
. In those three miles the elevation changed some 600 feet and exposed a wide variety of geological formations.

Mr. Summers had suggested that this canyon would be interesting; we found it to be that and more. We encountered one unusual rock formation after another. In places vertical walls nearly closed the canyon and one could only imagine the fantastic currents when flash flooding occurred. Where the walls opened wider, we discovered great natural amphitheaters that could project a whisper for a surprising distance.

We saw overhangs capable of sheltering a fair-sized mobile home, while others were barely large enough to hide a rabbit. Once in a while, coal seams would surface and provide a striking contrast to the pastel sandstones that made up much of the terrain.

We collected samples off the bedrock from both the main channel and from ravines that emptied into Squirrel Canyon. While the others did this, I moved the metal detector over much of the same ground. I received nothing for the effort until we moved far up the gulch near its head.

Then, in the course of three hundred yards, the detector sounded off three different times. Each time, I dug down in the channel for about a foot, spread out the material, went over it carefully, but found nothing. The only thing I could think of at the time was ground mineralization. Terry said she thought it was the operator. Looking back now, I think she was probably right.

The most interesting thing that happened that day occurred as we were coming back down the canyon late that afternoon. Cliff had climbed up out of Squirrel Canyon to a series of tables that lay to the east of the main channel. Inez, Terry, and I had stopped to rest for a few minutes and I took the opportunity to walk downstream about fifty yards to a place that looked as if it would become a waterfall in wet weather.

After I had checked this out and started back to where the girls were, I noticed a slight cavity to the left of a towering column of sandstone. The sandstone column, part of the canyon wall, looked to be forty to fifty feet high. Over the years, Terry and I had seen this situation many times, and it usually turned out to be just the way it appeared in the beginning—a slight cavity. This time, however, was one of the exceptions.

The first narrow vestibule, half full of tumbleweeds, simply led into another, and that into still another, following a pattern something like an S-curve on a highway. Trees, weeds, and boulders were everywhere. The going was difficult, but I was determined to see where the narrow passage would come out.

I expected any minute to see the ever-rising terraces that would mark the end of the winding gulch; instead, it went on for about a hundred yards to where it opened up into quite a valley. My heart pounded as I looked out across the picture perfect scene.

Across my mind went the fleeting thought, *Dear God, have I walked through the Little Door itself?*

There was a little rise in front of me, which I ascended to get a better view of the valley. A winding creekbed came from the upper end of the basin and followed a course right down through the passageway that I had used. I had left the metal detector back at the first entrance, so I decided to get it and bring the girls back with me to see this place. I thought about that morning and how none of us had seen the peculiar entryway. We had walked right by it. When I got back to Squirrel Canyon, I walked downstream a few yards and turned around.

Even knowing where that entrance was did not help much. A person had to be looking directly at it as he approached from the front in order to see it.

Inez and Terry were impressed; as they followed behind me I heard them talking about the Little Door. They were also surprised when they saw the picturesque valley and its winding creekbed. The creek was dry and sandy now, but it was obvious that it once had carried a good stream of water.

Inez spotted a pile of rocks on the side of the valley, about two hundred yards from where we were standing. Having seen it too, I told her I would check it out. I wanted to go to the upper end of the valley and come back along the creek with the metal detector.

The rocks, however, proved to be no more than a natural outcropping, not the remnant of a long-fallen fireplace. The bed of the creek was an equal disappointment; I spotted several coal seams, but no prominent veins of gold. The samples taken from the area, did contain traces of gold.

After they had gone back down the passageway, I stood looking at the little valley. It was surrounded by ridges and tablelands, and that made it fit the description of the canyon Adams had talked about so many times. It was complete with the zigzag crack through rock walls, just like the Little Door of the legend. As I studied the jumbled maze stretched out before me, I wondered how many more situations there were like this? It was another one of those profound questions that would creep back while I made an effort at understanding not only the legend but this incredible country as well.

The second morning, we took a canyon nearer our camp to explore for gold. I noticed as we left the campsite that a few clouds had gathered along the western horizon.

Cliff noticed them too, saying, "I hope those clouds don't get over this way."

I agreed and added that I did not think they would amount to much. Just then, we spotted an eagle flying down the canyon, and for a time the clouds were forgotten.

Coal Canyon was not the narrow gulch that Squirrel Canyon had been. For one thing, Coal Canyon was much wider and had more side canyons coming into it. Our crew could easily spend a number of days checking out this one canyon's drainage areas. As we looked at the terrain, it was not difficult to understand the forces of nature that created these canyons. Because of the vast watershed made by the coming together of so many ravines, tremendously powerful water flows would be generated by any sudden summer shower. The evidence of that power was everywhere in Coal Canyon.

Walking along, we saw clumps of sage brush as well as great pine trees clinging precariously to the edge of eroded canyon walls. It represented a change that takes place quickly and leaves nothing untouched. Narrow passages, such as the one we had gone through the day before, can be created or destroyed during the course of one summer of monsoon rains. A canyon that had once been effectively closed by the rush of fallen trees, brush, and boulders—the result of flash flooding—can also be opened up once more by those same natural forces.

This was the subject of our conversation while the four of us walked along Coal Canyon. It occurred to me that what we were talking about was just another example of the *Changing Arrows*. In this case, the changes were environmental and natural, and because of those natural changes, some of the things Adams once talked about may no longer be as he described.

We worked our way upstream, about a mile and a half, and entered one of the side canyons. At that point the walls had closed in and formed a box canyon that all but blotted out the sky. Suddenly, a loud clap of thunder set us all to looking at one another. The sky overhead, what there was of it, was clear and blue, but there was no mistaking what we had heard. It was thunder, all right!

We made the logical decision that, if it was going to rain, it would be best to get out of the canyon as quickly as we could. We barely made it back into the wider valley of Coal Canyon before it started sprinkling. Twenty minutes later, that sprinkling had developed into a heavy rainfall; to add to the situation, lightning was flashing all around us.

In our haste, we had passed up a dozen good overhangs, and now there were none to be seen. Finally, we found what looked like a good possibility. We pulled up under it onto a narrow ledge, out of the cold, wet rain. We were as happy as kings—right then. Soon the relatively dry sandbar we had crossed to get to the ledge became overrun by flooding water; at the same time, the clouds opened up, sending rain down in torrents.

Somewhere on the tableland far above us, a natural dike gave way sending thousands of gallons of water over the top of the rocky overhang under which we stood. There we were, on a narrow ledge, behind a great waterfall. Then, just when I was thinking that matters could not get much worse, a four-foot-long, green, mountain rattlesnake landed on the ledge. Fortunately, it dropped on a part of the ledge between where Terry and I were standing, and Inez and Cliff.

Cliff had a long walking stick that he had picked up earlier that morning, and now he used it to toss the snake out across the canyon.

Glancing over my way, he said with a grin, "There might be better places!"

Just as I was agreeing with that idea, another snake landed on the ledge. Needing no further encouragement, we were all looking for that better place.

For about a hundred feet we were in knee-deep water, the rain coming down in sheets. By that time, there was no way any of us could have become any wetter.

By then, the mouth of Coal Canyon had become a bank-to-bank current of fast-moving, sandy colored water. Still, it was nothing compared to the raging flood churning its way through the basin of Wild Horse

Canyon. Getting back to our camp turned out to be quite a chore since there was no wading across those currents. We were glad that our campsite was on high ground, well above the channel taking care of the runoff. At that moment, it looked as though the runoff could take several days.

The rain stopped about five o'clock that evening and it cleared some. We talked it over and decided that if it had not cleared completely by morning we should get out of that canyon area. We did not want to be caught there indefinitely. With the rain that had already fallen, our dirt road was saturated badly.

At sunrise the next morning, there was the sun, big and bright. It lasted all of fifteen minutes before dark blue rain clouds obscured it for the rest of the day. We knew it was only a matter of time, and not much at that, until it rained again.

We broke camp, putting everything away as fast as we could, and got ready to go. Before leaving, I walked a few yards away from the campsite to where I could see the basin of Wild Horse Canyon. There was no running water. In fact, it was as though it had never rained. The runoff during the night had been complete, but our frail roadway was something else again.

We made it about a mile, about halfway to the county road, before it started to rain again. Our dim, seldom-traveled track turned into a slick, gummy clay, and as we approached one of the long inclines, we were prevented from going any farther. The rain continued for several days and we probably would have been stuck there if it had not been for some quick thinking by Mr. and Mrs. Summers.

They called the King Ranch foreman, who was closer to us, and asked him to check on us. He came in the midst of a steadily increasing rainfall. Maneuvering his four-wheel-drive pickup in a manner second to none, he managed to pull us out. His name was John Lee, and he told us that if he had not reached us when he did, he would not have been able to help.

Thus, we received firsthand experience at how helpless people can be in that region during wet weather, when they are there without the benefit of four-wheel-drive vehicles. When it rains enough, and it does at times, even four-wheel-drive will not help.

Later, at Reserve, we had time to talk this over among ourselves and wonder how many times searchers in the past had been adversely affected by inclement weather. Did it make the difference when one of those searchers had come very close?

Weather was once again a factor as winter descended upon us. We promised ourselves that next spring we would try again.

The severity of a New Mexico winter depends to a large degree on the jet stream. When it holds a pattern across the southern part of the United States and therefore across New Mexico, our weather tends to be stormy with one cold front after another. There are times, though, when the jet stream moves far to the north; this results in warmer temperatures and Indian summer days. During such periods while 1983 became history and 1984 was becoming a reality, Terry and I made several more trips to the Summers Ranch.

It was on one of those trips when I called Mr. Summers *Mister* once too often. He told me he was *Henry* or *Henry Lee,* and he added, pointing to Mrs. Summers, "Call her Clyde."

As I looked into Clyde's smiling face, I was glad he had said that. It felt strange being formal with people with whom we were otherwise so comfortable. After that, it was Henry Lee and Clyde.

The conversation described above took place over early morning coffee, and a little while after that Terry and I left the ranch house to spend the day in the canyons. It was getting along toward evening when we pulled back into their yard. On these trips, we made it a point to go by the house and let them know we were leaving the ranch.

Clyde came to the door and called out, "You'all come on in now. I've got supper almost ready."

We were in for a real treat. Clyde had prepared a big pot of her fine chile and beans, and Terry and I had just put in a long day in the wilds. The meal really hit the spot. That was the way it was with Clyde; she liked Terry and me, and went out of her way to make us feel at home. So did Henry Lee.

After supper, Henry Lee asked if he had ever told us about a stone carving on the ranch. He called it the *Lady on the Rock*. Before he brought up the subject of the carving, our conversation had been on the early Spanish expeditions that once moved through the area near the *Point of the Malpais*. We talked about Coronado's camp at the Point. Oñate was another conquistador who had explored in the area and there were others. Our discussion about the Spanish part of New Mexico's history had reminded him of the carving.

He said the figure was carved or scratched on a large slab of sandstone in the likeness of a woman, and that she appeared to be wearing a dress from some bygone era. The apparel seemed early Spanish to him. As interesting as the subject of the carving was, it would be some time before Terry and I would see it.

Once more our endeavor was halted by winter, followed by spring weather conditions that made it all but impossible to go to the ranch. It was July when Terry and I finally got there. When we did, the first thing we wanted to see was the *Lady on the Rock*.

Henry Lee offered his four-wheel-drive pickup for the short trip from the house. He thought our car might not make it.

A little while later, we stood looking at the strange artwork. My first impression was that of disappointment. The *Lady* did not appear to be very old. It looked to me as though someone had taken a rock of some hard substance, such as flint and scratched the image across the softer material of the sandstone.

Just as that was going through my mind, Henry Lee came up behind me and spoke.

"Now, the first time I ever saw that, it looked the very same as it does right now. If it has weathered any at all, I can't tell it."

"When was that? What year?"

"That was in nineteen thirty-three, the first time I was ever in this country."

I remembered then the signatures at El Morro; they had not changed much either—in several hundred years.

The image was on a flat, vertical wall of sandstone. At some point in the past, a fault had given way allowing the massive sandstone wall to split. As a result, a thick layer had sheared off leaving the flat surface. That surface was much lighter in color than the surrounding bluffs of sandstone; because of this, the flat wall on which the *Lady* was drawn could be seen for a long distance.

Across the top and exposed edges was the darker coloration of desert varnish. Desert varnish forms partly because of weathering, and its presence can be used to estimate the passage of time since the shearing occurred. The sheared-off portion, lying at the base of the vertical wall, appeared to have been there for a long time.

That, together with the desert varnish made me think that the sandstone canvas of the artwork was old indeed. Aside from this, I believed Henry Lee, and I think he was telling the truth when he said that the drawing had not changed in appearance in the more than fifty years since he had first noticed it.

I was interested in the *Lady* because she represented the work of someone in the distant past who had spent time in this isolated area. To me, there was always the chance that this might have something to do with the Adams mining expedition.

Even though one's first impression is likely to be similar to mine—that the image had not been there long—it is hard to explain the lady's garb. She would have been right in style in San Francisco during the days of the 1849 gold rush. Why would anyone draw her picture in this remote place in the latter half of this century?

We will probably never know the answers to the questions we have about the *Lady on the Rock*, but then it is only one of the mysteries of this beautiful and fascinating region—only one page in the lives of Henry Lee and Clyde Summers.

8

THE LAST OF THE
LANDMARKS

Although it is true that environmental phenomena could have produced changes capable of altering the appearance of some of the landmarks Adams talked about, there are a number of things to which he made reference that would not significantly change within the scope of five hundred or even a thousand years. Examples of this type of landmark include the general course of the rivers involved in the story, a double peak that can be seen for a hundred miles, the *Point of the Malpais,* and the two mountains that Adams said resembled haystacks. Those things will not change quickly.

Another landmark (mentioned in several of the accounts) could have disappeared as a result of natural forces or might well have lasted for hundreds of years. That landmark was the *aspen grove.*

Among the many versions of the Lost Adams legend, some address the happenings of the night of the massacres a little more closely than others. A book entitled *Old Magdalena Cow Town,* by Langford Ryan

Johnston, contains a chapter on the legend, and it would come under that heading.

Johnston is a son of the man who once spent many years searching for the Lost Adams bonanza with Captain Shaw. As that son, he had firsthand knowledge of his father's efforts. Indeed, at one point, he was a part of that effort himself.

In the part of his story dealing with the fateful night of the massacres, Johnston told how the terror-stricken Adams and Davidson defied fate and escaped the raiding Indians through a strange twist of luck. Later they hid themselves and waited for a wild victory celebration to finish, but the ordeal continued until three o'clock in the morning. The two survivors then gave up hope of being able to retrieve anything from the site.

The following is a quote from the Johnston text as it refers to the situation when the two men left the scene of the burning cabin.

> After walking for nearly two hours the approach of dawn drove them into hiding. They concealed themselves in an aspen grove and went to sleep.[1]

This book, *Old Magdalena Cow Town,* was not placed on the market until 1983. I did not become aware of it, however, until almost a year later when I acquired a copy and read the words quoted above. I had run across discussions about aspen trees in connection with the legend before this and now my interest in them was renewed. I went through the various accounts and discovered that reference to aspens occurred in many of the stories.

One of the accounts involving aspens was by a man named W. T. Tolbert. His story appeared in an issue of the *El Paso Herald* on August 13, 1927.

In this article, Tolbert relates the substance of conversations he once had with a man he refers to in the
text as being named Johnson.[2] The name Johnson—with
that spelling—is consistent throughout the article. In
the early 1920s, Tolbert had a ranch at the *Point of the
Malpais* and this man Johnson was one of his neighbors
who owned a place near the Datil Mountains, several
miles south of the Tolbert Ranch. A map contained in
the Tolbert article denotes the location of Johnson's
cabin, and it appears to be in almost the same location
as the *Johnston* homestead as that site is described by
Langford Ryan Johnston in *Old Magdalena Cow Town.*

Because of this, I believe Tolbert may have talked to
the old searcher, Langford Johnston. Perhaps the
spelling of the name in the article was made in error. Of
course, this is pure speculation on my part. There could
have been two totally different men with similar names
and similar stories.

The story Johnson told Tolbert was of an effort he
had made, for forty years, to find the gold of the Adams
strike. He claimed to have known Adams and to have
received vague instructions from him about the discovery site. Adams also told Johnson that he probably
would never find the canyon of gold because it would be
"next to impossible for anyone who had not been there
to find the place."[3]

At any rate, the Tolbert article places an *aspen
grove,* or as it is called in the article, an aspen *motte* out
in the cut-off and secluded area near the Summers
Ranch.

Gary Tietjen, in his *Encounter with the Frontier,*
explained how Jay McPhaul and others with him had
found an old rusted crosscut saw in a grove of quaking
aspen trees. Regarding the discovery of this saw and its
proximity to the gold strike, Tietjen asked two interesting questions. "Were they [Mr. McPhaul and those with
him] near the site and was this the saw that the provi-

sions party had lost?"[4] Apparently the saw had been lying in the aspen grove for a long time before it was found by Mr. McPhaul early in this century.

In one of my conversations with Henry Lee, I asked if he knew of any aspen groves in that area. He told me that there was one no more than a couple of miles away, just over a small hill from his house. That tied in with Tolbert's story. Tolbert, on the map he had included with his article, had located the aspen *motte* near a natural pond called Goat Tank. It was obvious that Henry Lee was referring to the same aspens.

To Terry and me, it was beginning to look as though this grove of aspen trees could be the important landmark that was not far from the end of the line. With that thought in mind, we planned another trip to the ranch to talk to Henry Lee and Clyde.

Henry Lee told us that the aspen grove we had discussed before was, in fact, the only aspen grove he knew of in that country from the Datil Mountains to the mountains far to the north. He went on to say that the grove was an old one, that it had been there long before he and Clyde moved into the area. He said initials and dates carved into the bark of those trees, some of which he remembered seeing years ago, dated before the turn of the century.

"There are dates visible right now that go back to the nineteen twenties," he added.

By the end of that conversation, Terry and I definitely wanted to see that aspen grove. Henry Lee said it was on his neighbor's land, but added that he did not think the man would mind if we walked in to it. He said we could drive part of the way and accordingly, an hour later, found us nearing the aspens.

We took along the metal detector, hoping to find some relic from the past, but if such a thing was there, we missed it. What we did find, nevertheless, was an unusual setting for an aspen grove.

In his book, Langford Ryan Johnston noted that Adams and Davidson had concealed themselves in an *aspen grove*. Other accounts told about the two men hiding for a time among aspen trees.

I wondered what it was about aspen trees that would make them a good hiding place. When we reached the aspens near Goat Tank, we found that hiding among them would be no problem. The grove is situated on the edge of a wide, sagebrush-filled valley, a wing or detached area off of what is called Goat Tank Canyon on the topographical maps. The aspens have sprung up among massive slabs of rock on the edge of the valley, and between the slabs, natural corridors provide perfect places to hide.

Some of the accounts tell about Adams watching from his hiding place and seeing Indians ride by scanning the ground for his and Davidson's tracks. The Indians found no tracks because where they were looking the ground was nothing but solid rock.

In our examination of this aspen grove, we found several acres of windswept sandstone adjoining the trees on the north side. As we walked away from the aspens, it crossed my mind that maybe another piece of this strange puzzle had fallen into place.

It had been an interesting day. The aspen grove we had seen was all one could ever expect the real grove to be if that part of the story was true. After walking through those trees, no one in our party had any doubt that the grove had been there long enough to be a part of the story. Some of the trees were of great size and obviously extremely old. Trees that were even older had died and fallen to the ground. The oldest date we found carved on any of the trees was 1923, and as Henry Lee had said, it was still easy to read.

One fact kept returning to me. *If those really were the aspens that Adams and Davidson had taken refuge in and they had gotten there in a matter of only hours*

Terry and the Aspen Grove

from the burning cabin, then the cabin site can't be far away!

In W. T. Tolbert's article, he said Johnson told him, that according to Adams, the two survivors had traveled for four or five hours in daylight before hiding in the aspen *motte.* Langford Ryan Johnston's account states that the pair fled the scene of the burning cabin at three in the morning.

There is quite a difference between running through the countryside in broad daylight for several hours and in creeping along for two hours at night. The fact remains, however, regardless of which of these accounts is true, the *aspen grove* is probably one of the final landmarks to be encountered before reaching the canyon with the gold. According to the old instructions, there was still one more.

Our trip from the aspens back to the ranch house took us over a high point. The topographical map of that area indicated that the high ground was a little over eight thousand feet. Further examination of the map disclosed that we were close to the divide that had kept us from seeing D-Cross Mountain and Bell Butte.

On our way to Grants that evening, Terry and I once more found ourselves analyzing the facts. It seemed as though everything was falling into place.

We had identified a trail that had connected this region with the Springerville area in 1864. If the Adams party had followed that trail away from the Springerville locale for as much as three days, they would have crossed another old trail, the one we believe is the wagon road of the legend. It would have taken the provisions party north to Old Fort Wingate.

East of the junction of these two trails, for a distance we judged to be about two days by horseback, there were two mountains that could well be the pair that Adams had once referred to as looking like haystacks. At a point only halfway between the two mountains and the crossing of the two trails, we had found a divide along which were several high places that would offer a splendid view of the possible haystacks. That divide could be approached only by long hours of upgrade riding such as was so carefully described by both Allen and Byerts.

Now, we had located an aspen grove only a little over a mile from the divide, and it was in the right direction from the divide to be the aspen grove of the legend. Suddenly, that divide seemed quite important.

The last of the landmarks could be there.

Cliff and Inez were due from Denver that next weekend, so we decided to wait for them and check out the divide together.

The Continental 727 rolled to a halt outside the satellite building that housed, among others, Gate 7 at the Albuquerque International Airport. Our gold hunting partners from Denver bore no similarities whatsoever to their nineteenth century prospecting counterparts as they deplaned the big jet.

Soon the four of us were crossing the Rio Grande River bridge, leaving Albuquerque behind as we drove west on Interstate 40 toward Grants.

Terry did most of the talking, telling Inez and Cliff about our latest adventure to the aspen grove. She also updated them on the most recent addition to our collection of publications on the Lost Adams, the book, *Old Magdalena Cow Town*. I told them I thought it contained one of the most important accounts that had been published on the legend. The fact that it had only recently been made available to the public added to the legend's enduring mystery.

That night, over enchiladas at a restaurant in Grants, we told them that we believed the *aspen grove* was one of the last of the landmarks. We thought we knew the general location of the last landmark that Adams had spoken of as being near the strike.

In most of the accounts and traditions, several facts never vary from one story to another. Along with the name Adams, the northeast course taken by the original expedition, the haystack peaks, and the gold canyon itself, there was the *high tableland* or *mesa*. From that *high mesa*, their guide had pointed out the two haystack mountains. He told the miners they had one more day's ride, toward the peaks, to the gold. Then, the guide led them off that *high mesa* and down into the canyon where they made their discovery.

It was also from part of that high mesa that Adams and Davidson watched the terrifying massacre of their comrades and saw what had been the dream of a lifetime die with them. This high tableland or mesa, part of a divide, was the last landmark. Somewhere near it, below it on the east side, is that special canyon, the mineral deposit, and the old hearth with its most unusual vault.

We all had a great case of gold fever as we traveled south along the faint, rough roadway after leaving the Summers ranch house. After passing the turnoff to the aspen grove, we turned a little to the southeast and started the uphill grade to the divide.

Henry Lee had told us that when we topped the hill we were now ascending, to stop and walk about a hundred yards east. From there, we would be able to see D-Cross Mountain and Bell Butte. I knew, by looking at the topographical maps, that from this angle the northern ridge of D-Cross would probably be visible, thereby revealing three summits instead of two. It was also evident by the maps that somewhere along this divide, the northern wing of D-Cross could line up behind the mass of Bell Butte, when it did, there would appear to be only two peaks.

A divide is simply a ridge of terrain that is higher than anything to either side of it. It is not unusual in this part of western New Mexico to find small tablelands or mesas scattered along these divides. Most of these flat-topped tablelands are only a few acres in size, and such was the case with the one we had just reached.

Henry Lee had called it a hill, and indeed that was what it appeared to be as our road approached it. Once on top, however, we found it to be one of a number of small plateaus in a string along the divide. The view both east and west was outstanding.

When he and Clyde had first moved into the area, Henry Lee found indications of several old trails along this divide. He said that the Indians had several routings through the area going in all directions. He also claimed that most of the canyons heading into the eastern rim contained springs and seeps of water.

Terry and I had been to some of the springs and seeps in other parts of the ranch. Onion Springs was one of those. We had also found the tiny seeps of water that would barely fill an eight-ounce cup in a minute's time. The four of us had been there when a sudden downpour had sent millions of gallons of water through the canyons; now, we stood on a divide that displayed the dynamic results of untold millions of years of erosion.

By then, we knew from our sample-taking that gold existed in the sandstone terrain that made up most of that country. This fact, and the way a person feels when he or she stands on that divide as we did, made us realize once again that the Adams story could well be true.

We stopped our vehicle and walked to the eastern rim of the tableland. Just as I suspected, D-Cross Mountain and Bell Butte gave the appearance of being three peaks instead of two. However, there could be little doubt that the farther south we went along the divide, the more the changing angle would present a view of two peaks, rather than three. The vast region to the east of us was extremely rough, with nothing but one ridge and canyon after another for miles and miles.

"It looks like the Painted Desert in Arizona," Inez said.

"Yes," Terry answered, "It really does."

I remember thinking how we could be reasonably close to the canyon of gold, but that it could still take a while to find it.

By looking far to the south, we were able to make out the low basin of Alamocita Creek where it lay winding from west to east toward the two mountains. We did not realize it then, but even that basin had a part in producing the illusion of the haystacks.

We spent our day checking those tablelands to the southwest. They seemed to be positioned from a quarter to a half-mile apart and each proved to be a little farther from our roadway. Each, therefore, took longer than the last to reach and ascend.

Sunset was about an hour away as we approached our last high point of the day. Once on top, we found the upper portions of D-Cross Mountain and Bell Butte were aligned about right, but the northern ridge of D-Cross was still quite obvious. To the southwest of our position were more tables along the divide. But the more we moved southward, the more the terrain toward the peaks became obstructed with points and ridges; some of those ridges had elevations approaching that of the divide, with the result that the dominance of the two mountains on the surrounding countryside was noticeably reduced.

While we stood watching, the entire panoramic view changed from one moment to the next. This came as a result of the evening sun as it settled lower in the western sky. I looked out across the vast and lonely region to the three summits and thought to myself, *That's one haystack too many.*

Quite a number of things had come together nicely to give us our theory, but the whole idea hinged on finding the two haystack mountains—not just any two mountains—those two!

I was certain that by the time we had come this far south, we would have lost sight of that northern ridge, but there it was. From our first trip down Alamocita Creek, the first time we had seen D-Cross Mountain and Bell Butte, the four of us knew that, when viewed from the right direction, only two peaks would be seen. I thought about that and how there must be a corridor extending westerly from the two mountains, a passage that would always show its travelers a scene with those two peaks in the east.

Maybe that's the answer, I thought, *and we're still not quite far enough south. There must be another table that is high enough, farther south along the divide.* Promising as it seemed at the moment, it wasn't long until this line of thinking was dropped completely.

We had worked our way around to the southern tip of the tableland, which at that point was not very wide. I turned and walked a few yards across the rocky surface to the western rim and looked to the west, back down Goat Tank Canyon. Several of the accounts tell about a worried Adams and Davidson—in the days just prior to the Indian attack—climbing to a high place where they watched down a long canyon for the returning provisions party coming from Fort Wingate. Even that fit, so well, the scene spread out before me.

Inez called, "Terrill, you're missing something!"

Although the light was fading fast, they were trying to get pictures of a quickly changing visual delight. The sun was low now, and the result on the eastern horizon was the dark blue signal of the approach of night. With an almost fragile simplicity, something happened that none of us had expected.

The great bell shape of Bell Butte began casting a shadow. Like a black ribbon, it spread itself over the base of D-Cross Mountain's northern ridge. Then, in a matter of a few minutes, that ridge simply disappeared into the dark blue background of the eastern sky. At the same time, the sun dropped low enough behind our divide to cause the divide to throw its shadow over all the rough country between us and the two peaks.

Because of the open basin of Alamocita Creek, nothing obstructed the rays of the setting sun from coming to rest on the two mountains. Straw-colored grasses across the slopes of the almost treeless hillsides picked up the reddish glow—and the entire scene was like a painting from the mastery of God himself. It was a truly fascinating thing to see.

The air hung still with not even the slightest movement that might have provided sound. Cliff's words, bearing a startled quality, broke the silence.

"Well, would you look at that!"

Terry was sitting on a rock ledge a little distance from me. She spoke next, her eyes glued to the distant peaks.

"There are your *haystacks*, sweetheart."

Inez agreed, adding, "They really do look like big mounds of hay!"

For a moment, we were all silent, our thoughts fully captured by the incredible sight.

"You know, this could happen only in August and September. In fact," Inez said, choosing her words carefully, "With the sunlight coming right down the creek basin, this will be seen only a few days each year."

Her point was well taken. The sun sets a little farther south each day in the late summer and fall. Only when it finds its way down through the valley of Alamocita Creek can this condition occur.

Then I had a thought and used it to join the conversation. "There is something else to consider—the weather. I'll bet there are some years when monsoon season clouds keep this from happening at all."

Cliff nodded his head in agreement.

As beautiful as it was, the illusion of the haystacks lasted for only a few minutes. Then the sunlight faded across the two summits and was no more. I believe this could have been what Adams saw on that August evening back in 1864, a stunning display of nature in one of her rarest moments. It might well be the sight that became so permanently anchored in his memory, a scene that has been looked for by so many for so long.

This is New Mexico to me. It is an incredibly beautiful state with visual treasures such as this that can change and become excitingly different with only the passage of minutes. When one takes this into consideration, it makes it a little easier to understand how this story has survived over the years, and why the gold may still be out there somewhere—just the way Adams and Davidson left it.

In the foreground lay the sprawling reaches of Harrington Canyon with its many side-entering ravines. The canyon of gold is possibly in one of these.

I glanced at Terry, then Inez, then Cliff. In their faces, I found the same question that was so much on my own mind. *Which canyon is it?* With little haste, the realization came to me that what we had just witnessed could have been observed from other tablelands we had been on that day.

Terry stood up and walked over to me. Looking to the west she said, "Oh! Look at that sunset! Isn't it magnificent?" Then turning to face me, she took hold of my arm and smiled. It was that same excited smile that had brightened her eyes when we spotted those faraway points of Veteado. She spoke with the same urgency she had used then. "We're close now, aren't we?"

"Yes," I said. "I think we are, but our search isn't over yet. I think we just found a *new* threshold!"

Indeed, a great treasure is out there waiting to be rediscovered. Conservative estimates by the Adams party placed the 1864 value of the gold in the hearth vault at $90,000. That was when gold was bringing about twenty dollars an ounce. Today, that same gold would be worth in excess of two million dollars. If it has been found, that fact has not been acknowledged by anyone in the Southwest.

There are two rich accumulations of gold in the canyon—the first, a natural deposit possibly worth hundreds of millions; the second composed of mined nuggets and dust, the treasure of that ill-fated group. It is hard to believe that one of these might have been found and the other left as it was. Those better odds are that both are still there, passed by and almost forgotten by the human race. Their place of residence is no more than *Four Days from Fort Wingate.*

EPILOGUE

When I began writing this narrative, I did so because of the conviction that I had become involved with one of the most fascinating stories that has ever come out of the Southwest. There was no way to know then that Terry and I would meet so many interesting people, some of whom we would come to regard as close friends. Part of this book is their story and the story of hundreds of people, from four generations, who were caught up in this appealing tale of mystery and gold.

The unusual interest in that appealing story began with the account of a great natural treasure that was once seen by the eyes of mining men. Then it was lost, never to be seen again. The mystery is here in this last fact. How could a vast hoard of raw native gold stay lost? In his book, *Apache Gold and Yaqui Silver,* Dobie asked the question, "In the malpais or out of the malpais, why can't the gold be found?"[1]

I believe he may have reached part of the answer when he was quoted in the *El Paso Herald-Post* on September 21, 1937: ". . . if they [the Lost Adams

Diggings] do exist, they are in a much larger country than I at first thought."

Now, fifty-seven years later, Terry and I will agree with Mr. Dobie. The sheer immensity and complexity of the region where Adams found and lost his great strike form a big part of the answer, but there is more to it. Another part of that answer lies with those who have looked for the lost gold mine and in what they expected to find.

One of the things about this story that stirs the soul of adventure in people is the usage of words in the old accounts to describe the strike and those who found it. Phrases such as "nuggets as large as hen eggs," "quartz laced with yellow metal," and "you can load a burro down with gold in one day's picking" were part of it. So were the descriptions of the miners when they realized what they had: "deliriously happy," "shouts of joy filled the canyon," and "we're all millionaires!"

Were they exaggerated? Probably. As a result, I think it would be fair to say that almost everyone who has looked for the lost strike has been looking for it with something of the exaggerated in mind rather than the realistic.

When it comes to understanding what it was that Adams and his fellow adventurers found, I like to go back to the Allen Account. As I have made previous references to the German who survived, please bear with me now while I bring up his story again in a different context. The following is a quote from the Allen Account.

> When the nine men went out for supplies, this German went with them saying that from where the supply party left the trail he wanted to travel, he would go on alone. The German took with him sixty-three pounds, three ounces of gold which he had panned out in eleven and one-half days . . . [2]

Allen goes on to say that the amount of gold was established by weighing it on a Yuma storekeeper's counter scale. With counter scales registering a pound at sixteen ounces, the German's sixty-three pounds and three ounces figures out to 1,011 ounces of gold. Divide that by eleven and a half days and it comes to just under eighty-eight ounces of the yellow metal per day. That is pretty good, but eighty-eight ounces is five and a half-pounds, and that is far from a burro load.

It seems to me that the important thing here is the eleven-and-a-half days it took him to get his gold. This fact alone takes down much of the exaggerated jargon. However, people believe what they choose to believe, and as long as the story of the Lost Adams exists, there will be those looking for the extreme. A few of them will probably walk right through the Adams canyon itself.

As I approach the end of my story, I would like to say we had found the old mine, but that is not the case. I can say, without reservations, that Terry and I have had a most enjoyable time of it. What we did find was adventure in its most appealing form. We have had a first-rate look at New Mexico, its history, its people, and its great natural beauty. We took much pleasure in the story of the Lost Adams and in our search for its treasure.

What we offer here is an idea, a theory, about that long-lost location. Our theory is the result of many years of exploration and research. Terry and I are strongly committed to the proposition that the legend is true. It is our dream to walk in the canyon that once knew the riches of both passion and gold. In so doing, we will walk through history itself.

A good deal of time has passed since our party of four watched the sun set across D-Cross Mountain and Bell Butte. The adventure is, however, still very much alive. Our team continues to prospect the rugged canyon areas to the east of the divide. The effort goes forth, that is, when weather and road conditions permit. We have worked a number of canyons, in a hit-or-miss pattern, from Tachado Mesa to the mouth of Harrington Canyon. In that region, every sample we have taken has assayed some gold, and most have shown the presence of silver— not much of either metal, but enough to indicate the definite possibility of scattered accumulations such as were spoken of in the legend.

The hit-or-miss pattern is far more miss than it is hit. We only touch about one canyon out of maybe fifty. Still, the odds are as good, if not better, than what one will find in Las Vegas. The jackpot could be much, much greater.

I am convinced now that we are right, but I am also wiser as a result of our effort. The truth is, there are many places in this lonely region where Adams could have found his gold. We have only scratched at the door. I would like to find the old cabin site and perhaps someday we will. In the meantime, we have the thrill of the quest and the hope that Terry and I can still take that most interesting walk.

. . . till then . . .

BIBLIOGRAPHY

INTRODUCTION
1. Williams, W.W., "Lost Placer Gold Mine," *Denver Times* (Denver, Colorado), February 19, 1899.
2. Byerts, W.H., "A Lost Mine Richer Than Solomon's or the Klondike," *El Paso Herald* (El Paso, Texas), February 19, 1916.
3. Mitchell, John D., *Lost Mines of the Great Southwest* (Glorieta, New Mexico: The Rio Grande Press, originally published in 1933).
4. Allen, Charles, *The Adams Diggings Story* (El Paso, Texas: a pamphlet published by the Hughes–Buie Company, 1935).
5. From *Apache Gold and Yacqui Silver* by J. Frank Dobie. Copyright 1939 by J. Frank Dobie. By permission of Little, Brown & Company.

CHAPTER 1. THE LEGEND
1. Allen, Charles, *The Adams Diggings Story.* El Paso, Texas: Hughes Buie Co., 1935.
2. Tenney, A.M., Jr., "El Pasoan Learns Story of Famous Lost Diggin's from Adams Partner," *El Paso Herald* (El Paso, Texas), December 24, 1927.
3. Ibid.
4. Allen, Charles, *The Adams Diggings Story.*
5. Kemp, Ben W. and Dykes, J.C., *Cow Dust and Saddle Leather.* (Norman, Oklahoma: University of Oklahoma Press, 1968).
6. Ibid.
7. Tenney, A.M., Jr., "Lost Diggin's."
8. Dobie, J. Frank, *Apache Gold and Yaqui Silver* (Boston: Little, Brown & Co., 1939).
9. Allen, Charles, *The Adams Diggings Story.*
10. Byerts, W. H., "A Lost Mine Richer Than Solomon's . . . "
11. Allen, Charles, *The Adams Diggings Story.*
12. Dobie, J. Frank, *Apache Gold and Yaqui Silver.*
13. Byerts, W.H., "A Lost Mine Richer Than Solomon's . . ."

CHAPTER 2. THE SURVIVORS
1. .Dobie, J. Frank, Apache Gold and Yaqui Silver.

2. Allen, Charles, *The Adams Diggings Story.*
3. Tenney, A.M., Jr., "El Pasoan Learns Story . . . "
4. Kemp and Dykes, *Cow Dust and Saddle Leather.*
5. Dobie, J. Frank, *Apache Gold and Yaqui Silver.*

CHAPTER 3. THE FACTS—A CLOSER LOOK
1. Byerts, W.H., "A Lost Mine Richer Than Solomon's . . . "
2. Ibid.
3. Ibid.
4. Allen, Charles, *The Adams Diggings Story.*
5. Byerts, W.H., "A Lost Mine Richer Than Solomon's . . ."

CHAPTER 4. NEW MEXICO AND GOLD
1. Minge, Ward Alan, *Acoma: Pueblo in the Sky* (Albuquerque: University of New Mexico Press, 1976).
2. Bancroft, Hubert Howe, *History of Arizona and New Mexico, 1530–1888* (San Francisco, CA: The History Company, 1889; Albuquerque: Horn & Wallace Publishers, facsimile by, 1962).
3. Northrop, Stuart A., *Minerals of New Mexico* (Albuquerque: University of New Mexico Press, 1959).

CHAPTER 5. THE SEARCHERS
1. Hand, Tisdale A., "The Woolsey Expedition" in *The Arizona Miner.* Prescott: Tisdale A. Hand, 1864.
2. Allen, *The Adams Diggings Story.*
3. Tenney, A. M., Jr., "El Pasoan Guides Two Parties in Search for Supposedly Rich Lost Adams Diggin's." *El Paso Herald,* 14 January 1928.
4. Dowling account in, "Story of Rich Placer as Adams Related it; Others Have Sought It." *El Paso Herald,* 2 July 1927.
5. McKenna, James A., *Black Range Tales.* (Glorieta, New Mexico: The Rio Grande Press) Originally published in New York by Wilson Erickson, Inc., 1936.
6. Ibid.
7. Ibid.
8. Christilaw, George E., "End of the Adams Mine Search." *Albuquerque Daily Citizen,* 3 December 1888.
9. Kemp and Dykes, *Cow Dust and Saddle Leather,* 1968.

CHAPTER 6. OUR SEARCH—A MODERN ADVENTURE
1. Hand, Tisdale A., editorial column in *The Arizona Miner,* 1864.
2. Allen, *The Adams Diggings Story.*
3. Tietjen, Gary L., *Encounter with the Frontier.* Los Alamos, New Mexico: Gary L. Tietjen, 1969.
4. Ungnade, Herbert E., *Guide to the New Mexico Mountains.* Albuquerque: University of New Mexico Press, 1972.

CHAPTER 7. THE CHANGING ARROWS
1. Kemp and Dykes, *Cow Dust and Saddle Leather.*
2. Tietjen, *Encounter with the Frontier.*
3. Dobie, J. Frank, *Apache Gold and Yaqui Silver.*

4. Allen, Charles, *The Adams Diggings Story.*

CHAPTER 8. THE LAST OF THE LANDMARKS
1. Johnston, Langford Ryan, *Old Magdalena Cow Town.* Magdalena, New Mexico: Bandar Log, Inc., 1983.
2. Tolbert, W. T., "Prospector Spends 40 Years Hunting Lost Adams Diggings." *El Paso Herald,* 13 August 1927.
3. Ibid.
4. Tietjen, Gary L., *Encounter with the Frontier.*

EPILOGUE
1. Dobie, J. Frank, *Apache Gold and Yaqui Silver.*
2. Allen, Charles, *The Adams Diggings Story.*

INDEX